Letts

KS3
Success

English

Revision Guide

Age 11-14

Nick Barber

Contents

Reading

Writing

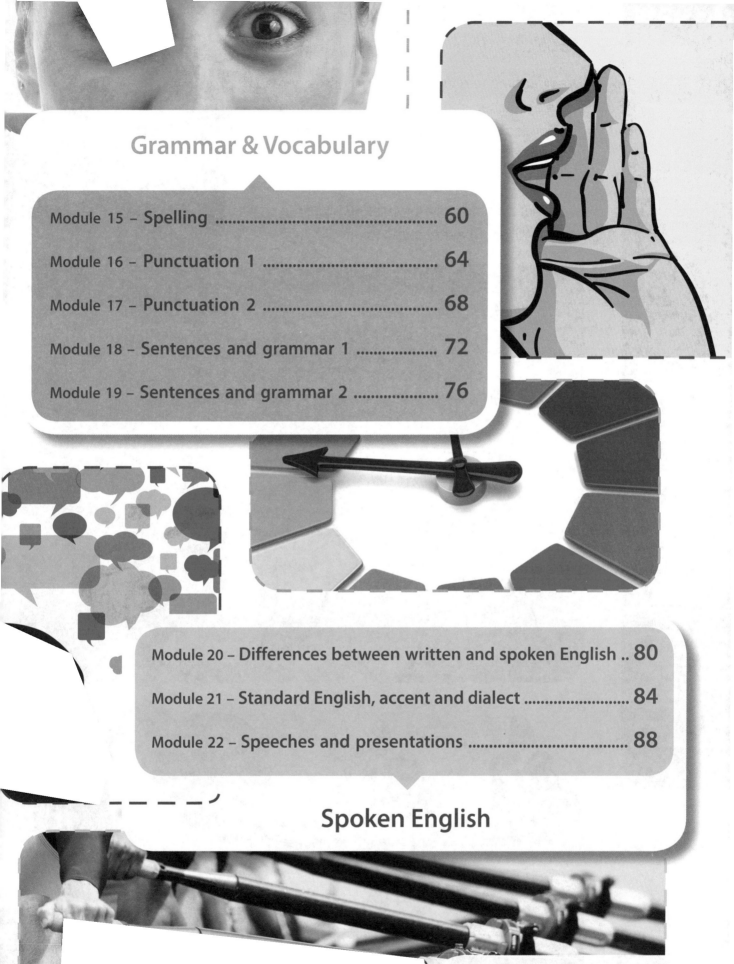

Grammar & Vocabulary

Spoken English

Background to Shakespeare

When reading and writing about prose, poems and plays, it helps to have an understanding of the times when they were written in order to gain a wider understanding of the writer's themes and ideas.

Important periods in literary history up to the time of William Shakespeare include:

Anglo-Saxon times

Not a great deal of Anglo-Saxon writing survives compared to other times – stories were only just being written down for the first time. Before this, many stories were told orally. Story-poems, like the famous **Beowulf**, were told with lots of **alliteration** and simple rhymes to make them catchy and easy to remember.

Beowulf (circa 1000)

The Canterbury Tales (circa 1390)

Le Morte d'Arthur (1485)

Romeo & Juliet (1597)

The Middle Ages

The most famous writer in the Middle Ages was **Geoffrey Chaucer**, who wrote *The Canterbury Tales*, a collection of stories told by pilgrims on their way to Canterbury Cathedral. Some are serious, some are very funny and some are regarded as quite rude. They are important, because as well as being entertaining, they tell us a great deal about people's lives, attitudes and beliefs in the Middle Ages.

Shakespeare and his contemporaries

Regarded by many people as the Golden Age of English Literature, the 16th and 17th centuries contained many important writers. **William Shakespeare** is the best known. He is important because of his success in writing in a wide variety of styles and his huge impact on the English language – many common expressions that we use today come from his writing, e.g. 'Love is blind'. Shakespeare wrote about all classes of people, from commoners to kings, as well as people and fantasy creatures from out of this world – no-one had ever written in such a wide range of styles before.

Other important writers from this time included **Ben Jonson**, who wrote plays and poetry and who, legend has it, used to enjoy debating with Shakespeare in London taverns. **Christopher Marlowe** was another contemporary, who might have gone on to produce a body of work to rival Shakespeare's if he had not been mysteriously killed in 1593.

There was a thriving theatrical tradition in London in the late 16th century. The Globe Theatre, which has now been rebuilt, existed at this time and burned down while one of Shakespeare's plays was being performed.

Another important writer in the Middle Ages was **Sir Thomas Malory**. His work *Le Morte d'Arthur*, a collection of stories and legends about King Arthur and the Knights of the Round Table and their search for the Holy Grail, is still well known today.

In Elizabethan times, the first dictionary had not been written and so writers were quite used to making up words and also rearranging sentences to make their writing more exciting. Elizabethan audiences were more sensitive to the subtleties of the language used by the actors. Perhaps more than modern audiences.

Alliteration ➤ Words close together, that begin with the same letter or sound

Write the names of each author mentioned in this module on separate pieces of paper. Write a fact about each, also on separate pieces of paper. Match up the authors' names with the facts about them.

1. Why isn't there a lot of Anglo-Saxon writing in existence?

2. How did the Anglo-Saxons remember their story-poems?

3. Name two writers from the Middle Ages.

4. Which centuries are regarded as the Golden Age of English literature?

5. Give two reasons why Shakespeare is important.

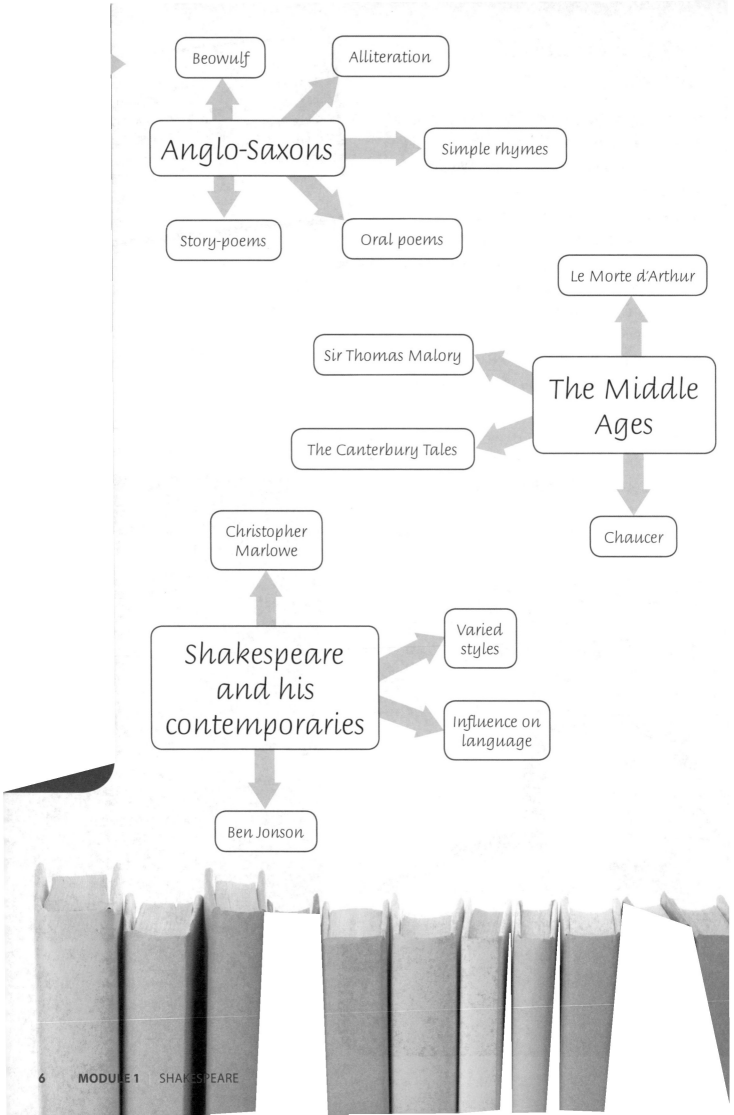

Beowulf

Alliteration

Anglo-Saxons

Simple rhymes

Story-poems

Oral poems

Le Morte d'Arthur

Sir Thomas Malory

The Middle Ages

The Canterbury Tales

Chaucer

Christopher Marlowe

Shakespeare and his contemporaries

Varied styles

Influence on language

Ben Jonson

Read the passage below and answer the questions that follow.

William Shakespeare (1564–1616) was born at Stratford-upon-Avon. His mother, Mary Arden, was one of the daughters of Robert Arden, a farmer; his father, John Shakespeare, was a glover and wool dealer of good standing who held an important local office. **1**

From the ages of seven to about 14, Shakespeare attended Stratford Grammar School. At the age of 18, he married Anne Hathaway, who was seven years older than him and three months pregnant. Her family owned a farm one mile west of Stratford. He lived with her until he went to London to become an actor. Some historians have suggested that he went away to London because he did not get on with his wife. Very little is known about Shakespeare's life around this time. Some people think that he must have travelled, in order to pick up ideas for his plays. He later became actor-manager and part-owner in the Blackfriars Theatre and later the Globe Theatre. **2**

Shakespeare belonged to the Lord Chamberlain's Company, where he was an actor. The company was renamed the King's Company in 1603 when James I became king. Among the actors in the group was Richard Burbage, one of the most famous actors of the time. **3**

Shakespeare returned to Stratford towards the end of his life. He died at the age of 52 on his birthday. He is buried in Holy Trinity Church, in Stratford. **4**

Questions

1. Name an occupation that Shakespeare's family were involved in. (1)

2. What does the phrase 'of good standing' suggest, in the first paragraph? (1)

3. What does the phrase 'an important local office' imply, in the first paragraph? (1)

4. Pick out and write down the sentence that gives a reason for Shakespeare moving to London, from the second paragraph. (1)

5. In the table below are paragraph summaries of the passage above. Write the paragraph number next to the correct summary. (4)

Paragraph summary	Paragraph number
This paragraph gives information about Shakespeare's membership of an acting company.	
This paragraph sums up Shakespeare's family background.	
This paragraph sums up the end of Shakespeare's life.	
This paragraph sums up Shakespeare's early life and the start of his career.	

Ways of building vocabulary

➤ Find books to read on your own. The more you read, the more new words you'll see, and the more you'll learn about language.

➤ Keep a dictionary by your side when reading to confirm any ideas you have about the meanings of new words.

➤ Look ahead in textbooks to learn new vocabulary and **concepts** before your teacher goes over the section in class.

Look at the situation (context) that words are used in – use that to help build your understanding of their meanings.

def·i·ni
The tea of the n

2

Prefix ➤ A group of letters added to the start of a word to modify its meaning

Suffix ➤ A group of letters added to the end of a word to modify its meaning

Root word ➤ The base word, after all extra parts have been removed

first

➤ Keep a list of key vocabulary specific to your study.

➤ Carry this list around with you – put it on a piece of paper or in a smartphone or portable device that you use a lot.

➤ Practise telling stories using the words 'first', 'then', and 'finally'.

➤ Talk about what you have read, using some of the new words you have found.

➤ Play word games – for example, try to use one new word a day at school or at home. Get friends to see if they can guess what the word of the day is, before you use it.

➤ Try to link less familiar words to words that you are familiar with – do they share similar **prefixes** or **suffixes** or **root words**? Could you build other words from these word parts?

➤ Use a thesaurus – in book form or online.

Vocabulary List

D

daughter
a girl or woman in relation to either or bot
parents.

decide/decision
come or bring to a resolution in the mi
consideration

definite
clearly stated or decided; not vague

design
a plan or drawing produced to sh
tion or workings of a building, g
before it is made

development
of developing or t

finally

Find 10 words in this book that you are unfamiliar with and write them down on a piece of paper or put them in a phone or personal device. By the end of tomorrow, use at least three in conversation.

1. How will reading improve your vocabulary?

2. What are prefixes?

3. What are root words?

4. Why should you read ahead in school textbooks?

5. How will a dictionary help you in your understanding of new words?

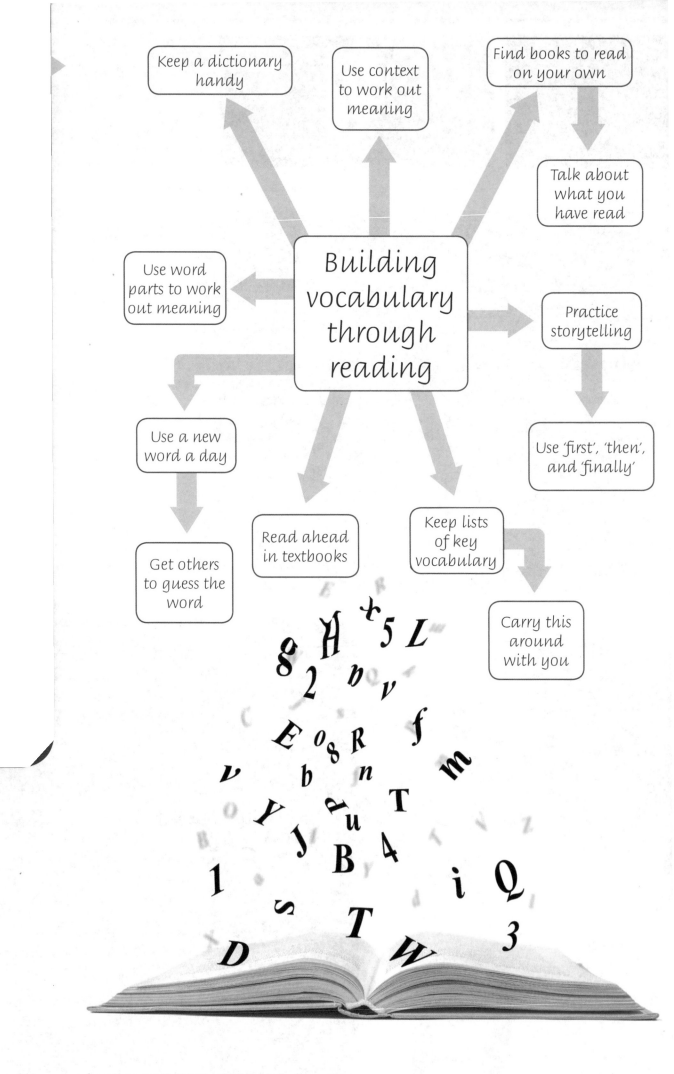

Keep a dictionary handy

Use context to work out meaning

Find books to read on your own

Talk about what you have read

Use word parts to work out meaning

Building vocabulary through reading

Practice storytelling

Use a new word a day

Use 'first', 'then', and 'finally'

Get others to guess the word

Read ahead in textbooks

Keep lists of key vocabulary

Carry this around with you

Read the passage below. Ten words are underlined. From the context of the passage and by relating the words to other words you may know, work out the meaning of each underlined word, from the choices available.

Cajun music is a regional <u>variation</u> of folk music from a variety of <u>sources</u>, including France, England, Nova Scotia and America. It is usually associated with Zydeco music, which is a similarly upbeat, <u>infectious</u> style of music made <u>primarily</u> for dancing and having a good time. Cajun and Zydeco music are played on traditional instruments such as accordions, many of which are made in the Cajun <u>heartland</u> by such builders as Marc Savoy and Junior Martin. Cajun music is sung in French or English. Cajun French is a <u>dialect</u> of modern French, that has more in common with the language spoken in France in the mid-18th century, when the original Louisiana <u>settlers</u> were expelled from French <u>territories</u> and came to live in the deep south of America. Many people from Louisiana are <u>bilingual</u>, using both their national and <u>historical</u> languages.

1. 'variation' in this passage means (1)
   a. type
   b. music
   c. group

2. 'sources' in this passage means (1)
   a. countries
   b. places of origin
   c. names

3. 'infectious' in this passage means (1)
   a. unhealthy
   b. catchy
   c. loud

4. 'primarily' in this passage means (1)
   a. mainly
   b. only
   c. always

5. 'heartland' in this passage means (1)
   a. hospital
   b. city
   c. the most important part of an area

6. 'dialect' in this passage means (1)
   a. a special variety of a language
   b. behaviour
   c. speech

7. 'settlers' in this passage means (1)
   a. foreign people
   b. people who move to live in a new country or area
   c. local people

8. 'territories' in this passage means (1)
   a. France
   b. areas
   c. countries

9. 'bilingual' in this passage means (1)
   a. can speak one language
   b. can only speak French
   c. can speak two languages

10. 'historical' in this passage means (1)
    a. boring
    b. old and traditional
    c. new

Reading between the lines is something you are expected to be able to do in order to go beyond straightforward understanding of a text. It is a sign of a more **sophisticated** reader. Reading between the lines can be developed by learning to question the text in front of you.

3

Look at this extract from *Romeo and Juliet*:

TYBALT   What, art thou drawn
           among these heartless
           hinds?
           Turn thee, Benvolio,
           look upon thy death.

BENVOLIO   I do but keep the peace. Put up thy sword,
           Or manage it to part these men with me.

TYBALT   What, drawn, and talk of peace! I hate the
           word,
           As I hate hell, all
           Montagues, and thee.
           Have at thee, coward!

Sophisticated ➤

Having a great deal of experience, advanced understanding and highly developed insight

Questions you might ask yourself

Here are some responses to questions about the extract opposite and further questions that they raise:

1. *What sort of mood is Tybalt in?* Angry, violent – why?
2. *Which words give you clues towards this?* "Turn thee", "look upon thy death" – why does he keep using commands? What else does this suggest about his character?
3. *Which punctuation gives you clues towards this?* Exclamation marks – why does Tybalt's character need to use so many? What does this suggest about how angry he is?
4. *What sort of mood is Benvolio in?* Calm, peace-keeping – why does he feel the need to do this? Is this his normal character?
5. *Which words give you clues towards this?* "I do but keep the peace" – why is he almost apologising? What does this suggest about how he feels towards Tybalt?
6. *What do the different moods of the two characters suggest about their relationship?* They don't get on? Why don't they get on? What's behind this?

The more questions you ask about texts, the more you will develop the skills of reading between the lines.

Think of three more questions you might ask about the extract from *Romeo and Juliet*. Write them on separate pieces of paper. Get some sticky notes and write suggested answers and match them with the questions.

1. **Why does reading between the lines make you a more sophisticated reader?**
2. **How can you develop your skills of reading between the lines?**
3. **Why, according to this module, might you ask yourself questions about punctuation?**
4. **Why, according to this module, might you ask yourself questions about the choice of words?**
5. **Why, according to this module, might you ask yourself questions about characters?**

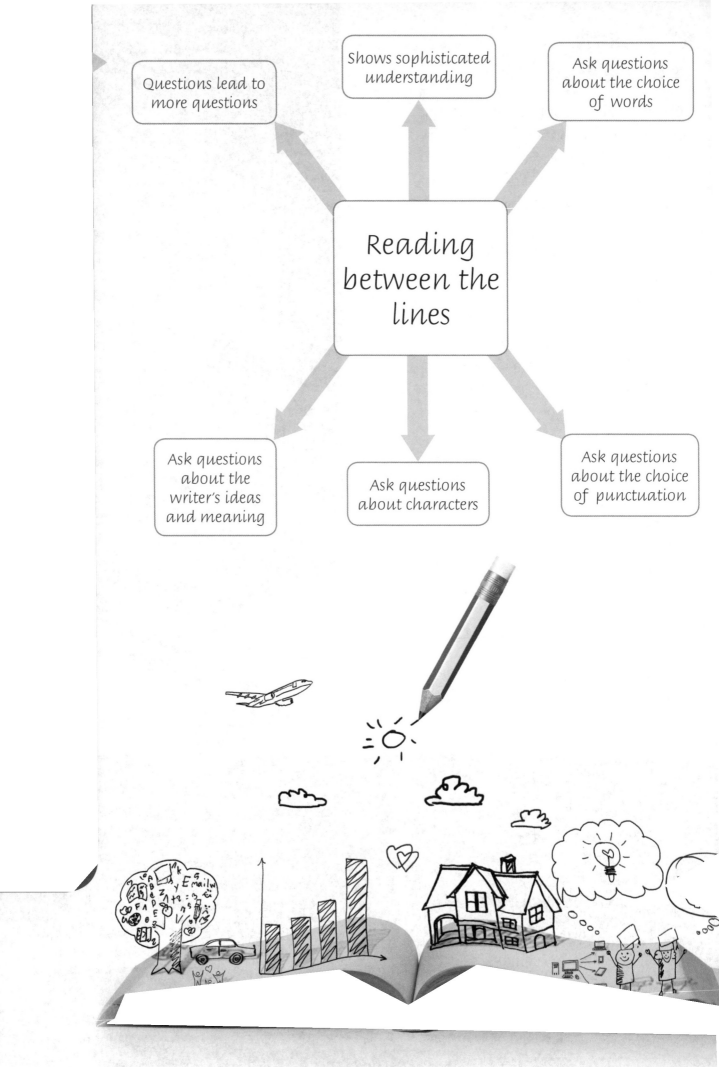

Questions lead to more questions

Shows sophisticated understanding

Ask questions about the choice of words

Reading between the lines

Ask questions about the writer's ideas and meaning

Ask questions about characters

Ask questions about the choice of punctuation

Read this passage. Think of two questions you might ask yourself about each of the underlined parts of the text. The first one is done for you as an example, in the table underneath the passage. Then put down suggested answers to your questions, in the third column.

From *Hard Times* by Charles Dickens

"NOW, what I want is, Facts. Teach these boys and girls nothing but Facts. Facts alone are wanted in life (1). Plant nothing else, and root out everything else. You can only form the minds of reasoning animals upon Facts: nothing else will ever be of any service to them. This is the principle on which I bring up my own children, and this is the principle on which I bring up these children. Stick to Facts, sir!"

The scene was a plain, bare, monotonous vault of a schoolroom (2), and the speaker's square forefinger emphasized his observations by underscoring every sentence with a line on the schoolmaster's sleeve. The emphasis was helped by the speaker's square wall of a forehead (3), which had his eyebrows for its base, while his eyes found commodious cellarage in two dark caves, overshadowed by the wall. The emphasis was helped by the speaker's mouth, which was wide, thin, and hard set. The emphasis was helped by the speaker's voice, which was inflexible, dry, and dictatorial (4). The emphasis was helped by the speaker's hair, which bristled on the skirts of his bald head, a plantation of firs to keep the wind from its shining surface, all covered with knobs, like the crust of a plum pie (5), as if the head had scarcely warehouse-room for the hard facts stored inside. The speaker's obstinate carriage, square coat, square legs, square shoulders, — nay, his very neckcloth, trained to take him by the throat with an unaccommodating grasp, like a stubborn fact, as it was, — all helped the emphasis.

"In this life, we want nothing but Facts, sir; nothing but Facts!"

1. Facts alone are wanted in life	Why does the speaker say this? What sort of character does this suggest he has?	It suggests that he's very opinionated and a bit dull.
2. The scene was a plain, bare, monotonous vault of a schoolroom		
3. the speaker's square wall of a forehead		
4. the speaker's voice, which was inflexible, dry, and dictatorial		
5. like the crust of a plum pie		

Audience

A text is affected by the audience it is written for – for example, Charles Dickens wrote many of his stories for magazines, in instalments, so he broke his stories into smaller parts, featuring many **cliffhangers**. This meant that the readers would want to buy the next edition of the magazine.

Purpose

A text is affected by why the writer has chosen to write it. A writer may have several purposes – for example, to entertain, to shock, to make people laugh, to make money, to communicate a point of view, or even just to work out their own thoughts and feelings. A text may have one purpose, many, or very little purpose at all.

The writer Thomas De Quincey decided that the only audience he would write for was himself. As a result, his writing reads like someone thinking out loud and talking to themselves.

Cliffhangers ➤
Parts of a story where the ending is not explained, so that the reader is made curious and wants to read the next part

Context

The time and situation in which a text is written will probably affect it. For example, the writer's gender might affect their opinions or point of view, as might where they live in the world, what they believe and what is going on around them at the time they are writing. A writer may be fitting in with a fashion or rebelling against it. The effect of context may be large or small – not all writers are influenced to the same degree by the world around them.

How might a person's life and appearance affect their writing? Find a picture of a person from a newspaper or magazine article and read a little about them. Stick the picture in the middle of a larger sheet of paper. Imagine that this person is a famous writer. Brainstorm, based on clues from his or her appearance and the details you have about them. What kind of stories might he/she write? (For example, if it's a tough-looking man, you might think he writes violent thrillers). Who might he/she write for? Why might this person have chosen to be a writer?

1. Give one way that the audience it is written for might affect a text.
2. Can the audience of a text be the writer of the text?
3. Name two reasons why writers might produce a text.
4. What might a writer's gender affect?
5. Name two ways that writers might react to fashions.

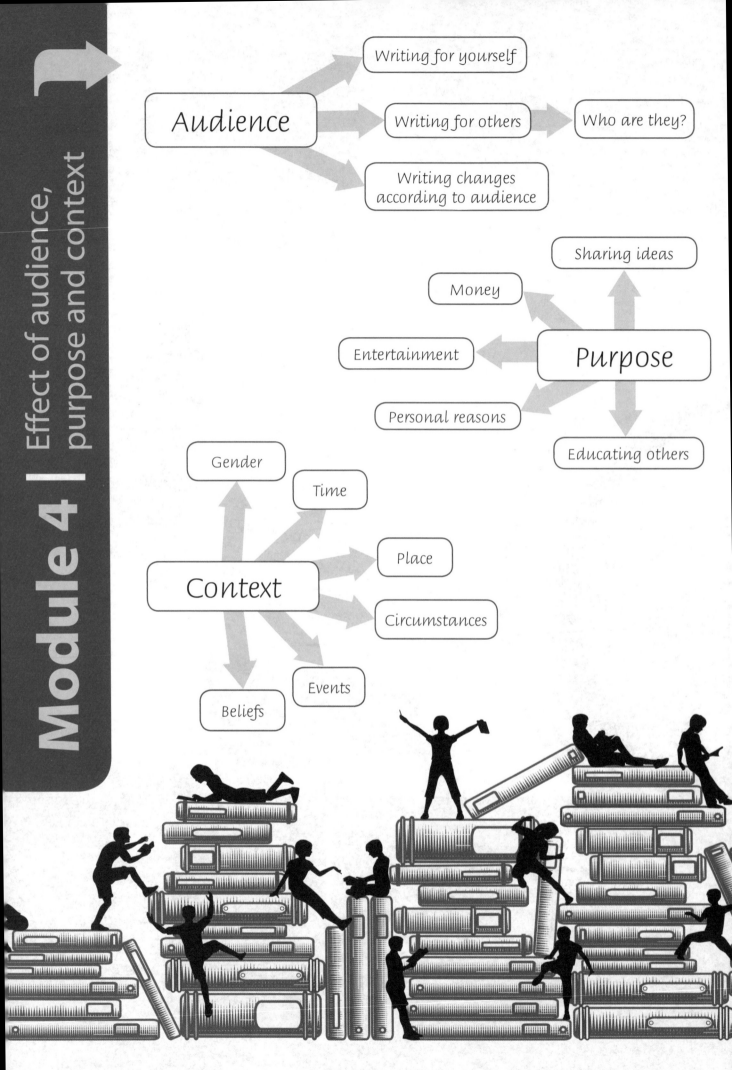

Audience

Writing for yourself

Writing for others → Who are they?

Writing changes according to audience

Purpose

Sharing ideas

Money

Entertainment

Personal reasons

Educating others

Context

Gender

Time

Place

Circumstances

Events

Beliefs

> Read the brief summary of Jane Austen's life and the brief summary of one of her most famous novels, *Pride and Prejudice*, and answer the question that follows.

Extract 1 – Jane Austen's life

Jane Austen was part of a large Hampshire family – Jane's father was a middle-class priest and was in charge of parishes in Steventon, Hampshire and Bath. Jane's closest family member was her sister Cassandra, with whom she shared all her thoughts and feelings and with whom she shared regular correspondence. When the Reverend Austen died, Jane, Cassandra and their mother were nearly penniless and had to stay with relatives for a while, before moving to a smaller cottage than they were used to, in Chawton, Hampshire. After Jane's death, Cassandra destroyed many of Jane's letters that related to her love life. It is believed that she had fallen in love with a doctor or other professional man while on holiday on the south coast around 1800, but he died and the relationship was thwarted. There is no proof of this, only family rumours which have been passed down the generations.

Extract 2 – *Pride and Prejudice*

The heroine of *Pride and Prejudice*, Elizabeth Bennet, is one of five daughters to the middle-class, but financially strapped, Mr and Mrs Bennet. Elizabeth is close to her sister Jane, who is regarded as the prettiest of the five daughters and, as the oldest, should be the first to marry. Mrs Bennet is worried about how long it is taking for her daughters to get married off, in order for them to achieve financial security. She fears that the family will not be able to survive with five daughters in their current home. When Mr Bingley arrives in the local area, Mrs Bennet's curiosity is sparked and this begins a series of events which draw Jane and Bingley and Elizabeth and Bingley's friend Darcy together. Elizabeth dislikes Darcy at first and his initial proposal is rejected by her, thwarting a relationship between them. It is only when events show that both Darcy and Elizabeth have made mistakes and they work to put them right that there is a happy ending.

How might Jane Austen's life have affected the purpose and context of her writing? (3)

Figurative language

Words can carry several layers or shades of meaning. When they do, this is known as figurative language.

Writers use various techniques to create different types of figurative language. These include:

➤ *comparison or relationship techniques* – similes, metaphors, personification, pathetic fallacy

➤ *emphasis or understatement techniques* – exaggeration, irony, hyperbole

➤ *figures of sound* – onomatopoeia, alliteration, sibilance, fricatives, assonance

➤ *verbal games* – puns, jokes.

Write the words 'onomatopoeia', 'alliteration', 'sibilance', 'fricatives' and 'assonance' on separate pieces of paper. Find and write down on the back of each piece of paper an example of that language feature . You now have several pieces of paper with an example on one side and a language feature on the other. Place the pieces of paper with the examples face-up. Try to guess the language feature from the example that you can see. Turn the paper over to see if you were correct.

Language can have a variety of meanings, depending on such things as:

➤ the situation the words are used in
➤ who says them
➤ their context
➤ how they are said.

Chronological ➤ Going in order of time

Form

The form of a text is all the 'ingredients' that writers of a genre use to make it recognisable. When thinking about a text, these are the characteristic features that are shared by other novels, plays or poems which make them what they are.

The form of a text is affected by ideas such as:

➤ *characterisation* – how characters are written and presented to portray certain ideas
➤ *use of settings* – places can influence the reader's understanding of the writer's ideas
➤ *use of time* – does the writing go in **chronological** order, or does it jump backwards and forwards?
➤ *genres* – biography, diary, letter, romance, science fiction, etc.
➤ *point of view* – who is speaking and why?

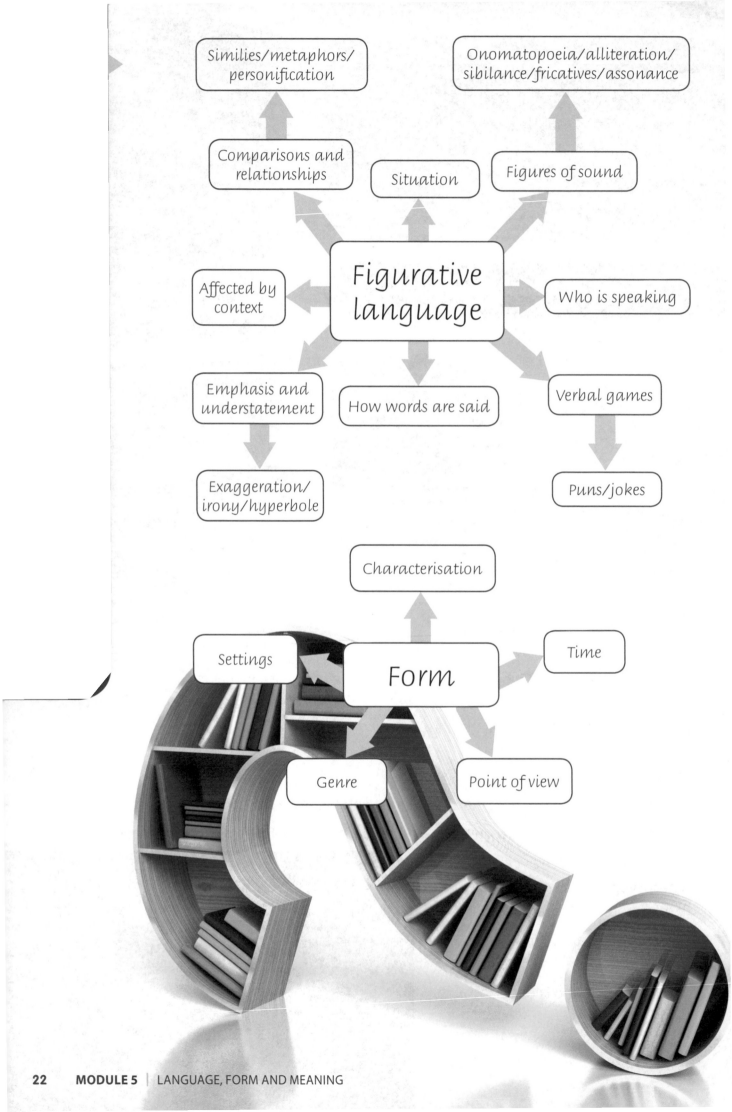

Similies/metaphors/
personification

Onomatopoeia/alliteration/
sibilance/fricatives/assonance

Comparisons and
relationships

Situation

Figures of sound

Affected by
context

Figurative
language

Who is speaking

Emphasis and
understatement

How words are said

Verbal games

Exaggeration/
irony/hyperbole

Puns/jokes

Characterisation

Settings

Form

Time

Genre

Point of view

Read the passage and answer the questions below.

I was shocked by what I saw – I'd seen nothing quite like this city, even though I'd read about it and seen it on so many films. The sheer scale of the skyscrapers that towered above my head made me feel intimidated and threatened. The noise of impatient drivers tooting their horns to get across town filled the dusty air and the lingering smells of pizza and a myriad of other odours – not all pleasant – assaulted my nose.

My first day in New York was frantic. I struggled to come to terms with basics like crossing the road, but loved the colours and noise, even if everyone seemed angry, aggravated and anxious, barking belligerently at the world. As night fell, the city took on a new life. Neon and strip lights filled the city with a variety of decorative illumination and every building contained its own warm oasis of light, safely away from the dark hostility of the street.

It took me a while to settle into the pace of life, but I came to enjoy the vibrance of the city. I saw the street as an ever changing soap opera. The petty arguments and the moments of beauty all filled my waking moments as I wandered around, almost anonymously, observing and taking mental notes for the task ahead.

I was on a photo assignment. I had been sent to the 'Big Apple' – New York – by a magazine, to document the changing face of the city. Quite how the magazine expected me to recognise how it had changed, when I'd never been there before, I wasn't so sure, but I wasn't going to complain. They were paying me to stay in the most exciting city on earth for two months and they were picking up the bill…

1. Which viewpoint is this passage written from? (1)

2. Find an example of alliteration and explain its effect. (1)

3. This is an extract from a biography. Other than the viewpoint it is written from, give one other feature of biographical writing that this passage contains. (1)

4. Pick out two phrases which show how the setting affects the writer. (2)

5. Which tense is this passage written in? (1)

6. What sort of style is this passage written in and what effect does this have on the reader? Use a quotation, or quotations, to support your answer. (3)

English poetry has five basic rhythms of varying stressed (/) and unstressed (x) **syllables**.

They are grouped into 'meters' called iambs, trochees, spondees, anapests and dactyls.

Syllable ➤
An unbroken sound used in groups, to make up words

Tiger! Tiger! burning bright,
In the forests of the night,

Rhythm

Each unit of rhythm is called a 'foot' of poetry.

Iambic: **x /**

Example: But, soft! what **light** through **yon**der **win**dow **breaks**?

A stressed syllable is written as / and an unstressed syllable is written as x, when marking out above a line's rhythm. In the examples, the stressed syllable is also in bold.

Trochaic: **/ x**

Example: **Pe**ter, **Pe**ter **Pump**kin **Eat**er

Dactylic: **/ x x**

Example: **Just** for a **hand**ful of **sil**ver he **left** us

Anapestic: **x x /**   Example: The As**syr**ian came **down** like a **wolf** on the **fold**

The number of times that a foot is repeated in a line gives the line a name too. For example, a line with five iambic feet is called 'iambic pentameter'. Shakespeare uses this rhythm a great deal.

Feminine rhyme – a rhyme in which the stress is on the second-from-last syllable of the words (e.g. picky, tricky).

Half-rhyme – matching final consonants (e.g. dent, ant).

Assonance – vowels that match (e.g. frail, grace).

Consonance – matching consonants (e.g. struck, reak).

Poetry does not have to rhyme, but many poems do. Rhyme can be used in different ways for different effects. There are many types of rhyme, but these are some of the main ones:

Masculine rhyme – a rhyme in which the stress is on the final syllable of the words (e.g. spent, went).

Rhyme

Rhyme patterns

Rhyme patterns are written as letters, e.g. this poem is **AABB** because the first and second lines rhyme with each other and the third and fourth lines rhyme with each other.

The dog ate his bone
But sat all alone
He wanted a walk
But alas could not talk

Copy these lines onto a piece of paper and number each syllable.

Now is the winter of our discontent
Made glorious summer by this sun of York;

This is an example of iambic pentameter, so its pattern is x / .

Read the lines out loud. Say each odd-numbered syllable quietly and each even-numbered syllable louder. This will help you to emphasise and recognise the rhythm.

1. What are the five main types of meter?
2. Which types of meter are based around two syllables?
3. Which types of meter are based around three syllables?
4. What is masculine rhyme?
5. What is feminine rhyme?

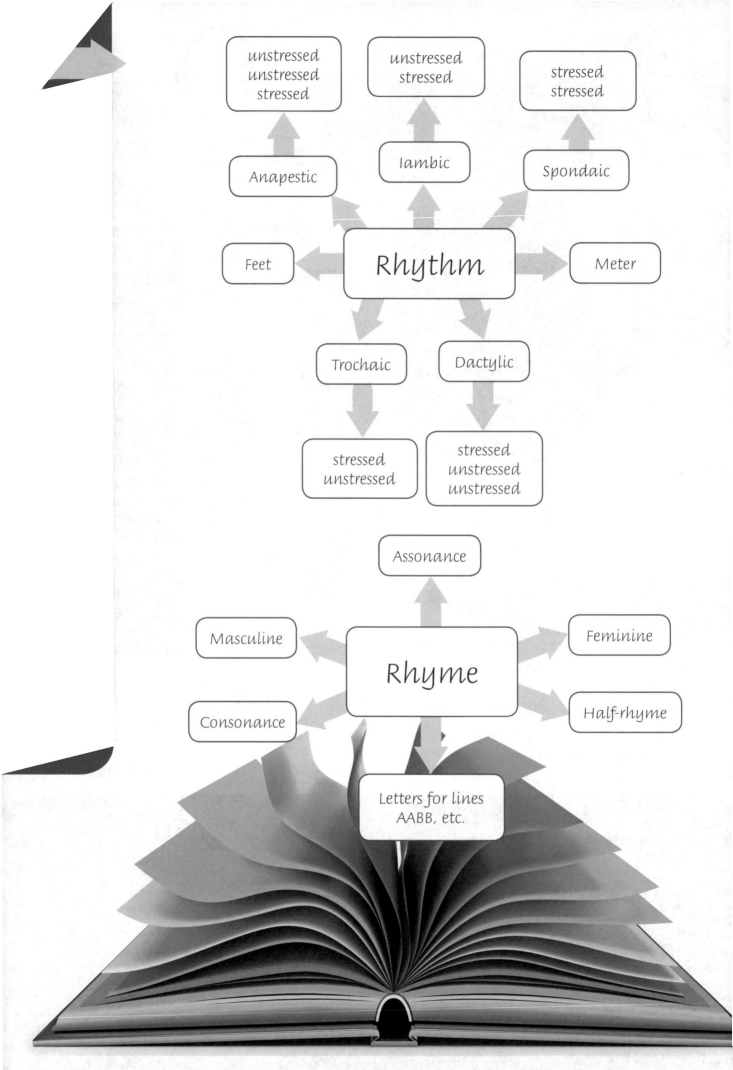

Answer the questions below.

1. **Rhythm**

   a. How many syllables are there in a line of iambic pentameter?   (1)

   b. How many syllables are there in a line of iambic tetrameter?   (1)

   c. What does 'meter' mean related to poetry?   (1)

   d. What does trochaic mean?   (1)

   e. What does anapestic mean?   (1)

   f. What does dactylic mean?   (1)

   g. What does spondaic mean?   (1)

   h. What type of rhythm is 'big deal' an example of?   (1)

   Read these lines – what type of rhythm do they contain?

   i. To strive, to seek, to find, and not to yield (Tennyson)   (1)

   j. With the odours of the forest (Longfellow)   (1)

   k. Be near me when my light is low (Tennyson)   (1)

   l. Half a league, Half a league, Half a league onward (Tennyson)   (1)

2. **Rhyme**

   a. Write down, in letters, the rhyme pattern of this poem.   (1)

   There was a young man from Stoke
   Who wrote some books as a joke
   He said "I'm a teacher,
   Not a judge, nor a preacher"
   And it's only because I am broke!"

   b. Write down, in letters, the rhyme pattern of this poem.   (1)

   Robin Hood was very brave
   He always seemed to win
   When fighting with the Sheriff's men
   He fought them with a grin.

Types of imaginative writing

Prose

- Short stories
- Factual prose
- Letters
- Novels
- Diaries
- Testimonials
- Journals
- Personal essays

Poetry

Acrostic	**Kennings**
Ballad	Limericks
Blank verse	Lyrics
Epic poems	Odes
Epigrams	Shape poems
Free verse	Sonnets
Haiku	

Drama

Scripts

Comedy

Tragedy

One-act plays

Pantomimes

Active voice ➤ Where the subject does the action determined by the verb: 'The hunter saw the deer.'

Passive voice ➤ Where the subject expresses the theme of the main verb: 'The deer was seen by the hunter.'

Kennings ➤ Where an object is described in a two-word phrase, such as 'sky dandruff' for 'snow'

On three sticky notes write the words 'Prose', 'Poetry' and 'Drama'.

On other sticky notes (preferably of a different colour) write down as many different types of imaginative writing as you can find on these pages, plus any more that you can find. Place the 'Prose', 'Poetry' and 'Drama' notes on a blank wall, as headings. Put the notes with the different types of imaginative writing on, underneath the correct heading.

Imaginative writing – general decisions to make

- Imaginative writing can be fiction or non-fiction. Many writers choose fictional forms as it can give greater freedom, because the writer is not tied to including facts.
- Who are you writing for? This will affect the formality and style of your writing – for example, someone writing for an adult audience will write differently to someone writing for young children.
- What purpose do you have in your writing, e.g. to entertain, shock, describe, etc.?
- Which genre or genres do you wish to write in or be influenced by?
- What sort of style, mood or tone are you going to use, and why?
- How are you going to use sentence lengths for effect?
- How are you going to use vocabulary for effect?
- Where is your writing going to be set, and why?

7

further things to consider

Imaginative prose

- Which viewpoint are you going to use?
- Are you going to write in the first or the third person, and why? Might you make use of the second person?
- Should you write in the active or passive voice?

Imaginative drama

- What style or genre of play are you going to write, e.g. comedy, tragedy, melodrama, etc.?
- What sort of performance space or medium are you going to write for, e.g. film, theatre, radio?

Imaginative poetry

- Which type or form of poem are you going to choose, e.g. sonnet, ballad, limerick, etc.?
- Does it need to rhyme?
- If it is going to rhyme, which rhyme pattern are you going to choose, and why?

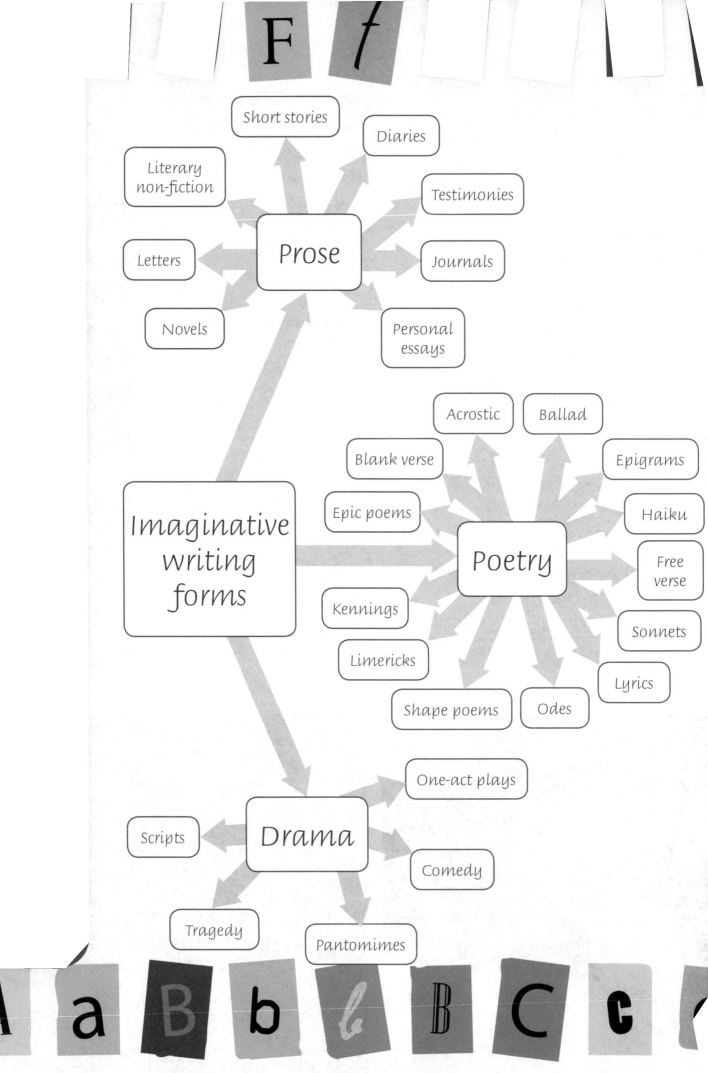

F f

Prose
- Short stories
- Diaries
- Testimonies
- Journals
- Personal essays
- Literary non-fiction
- Letters
- Novels

Imaginative writing forms

Poetry
- Acrostic
- Ballad
- Blank verse
- Epigrams
- Epic poems
- Haiku
- Free verse
- Kennings
- Sonnets
- Limericks
- Lyrics
- Shape poems
- Odes

Drama
- One-act plays
- Scripts
- Comedy
- Tragedy
- Pantomimes

A a B b b B C c

Answer the questions below.

1. Match the writing types to the features. (10)

Writing type	Features
Limerick	Dark settings, references to evil and the supernatural
Horror novel	A humorous play traditionally involving audience participation
Love sonnet	A play that has a very sad ending
Melodramatic play	A story-poem, usually of some length
Science fiction novel	A novel that may involve emotions of attraction
Pantomime	14-line poem usually written by an admirer
Tragic play	A novel that tells the life story of an imaginary person or character
Fictional biography	A novel that may involve futuristic ideas
Ballad	Short, five-line AABBA humorous poem
Romance novel	A play with extravagant action and emotion

2. Change these sentences, which are written in the active voice, into the passive voice.

    a. The boy ate his carrots. (1)

    b. The girl did her homework. (1)

    c. The singer sang his song. (1)

    d. The writer crossed out his mistakes. (1)

    e. The footballer kicked the ball. (1)

3. Change these sentences, which are written in the passive voice, into the active voice.

    a. The result was accepted by the manager. (1)

    b. The school was closed by the bad weather. (1)

    c. The tree was chopped down by the gardener. (1)

    d. The meal was cooked by the celebrity chef. (1)

    e. The television was switched off by the engineer. (1)

4. For each of these imaginative forms of writing, say whether they are poetry, prose or drama.

    a. Novel (1)

    b. Ballad (1)

    c. Diary (1)

    d. Letter (1)

    e. Short story (1)

Formal writing can be for a variety of purposes, but they all have the following features in common:

> The writing needs to be clear.

> It needs to be as literal as possible.

> It needs to be well-structured and organised.

> It needs vocabulary suitable for its audience.

> It can be written from a variety of viewpoints, but the passive voice is often a good choice, because it makes the writing less personal and biased – and therefore more formal.

Last Co

Monday

Types of formal writing

There are many types of formal writing. Here are some of the more common ones:

Business letters

Job applications

JOB APPLICATION FO

Educational or reference books

Academic essays

It is very important to consider the impression you are making on the audience in formal writing. In these examples, the writer needs to make a favourable impression on the reader:

> In business letters and job applications you might want to win a contract or a job

> In educational writing the ideas will need to come across as clear and well-structured and expressed so that you can gain credit in examinations, controlled assessment or coursework.

Formal letters

The rules for writing letters have changed over time and will continue to change. This means there are no definitive right or wrong rules, only generally accepted ones. For example, some companies have a house style of putting the sender's and the recipient's address on the same side. Others will put them on opposite sides. That does not mean they are wrong – just different. Some of the more common features of formal letters are listed here, but there are often variations on these in practice.

Formal essays

Depending on the subject and level of assessment, formal essays can take slightly different forms, but many of their shared qualities are as follows:

1. An introduction which addresses the issue to be discussed.
2. A series of points developing a line of argument, known as a thesis, backed up with evidence, often in the form of quotations, footnotes or endnotes, or all three.
3. A conclusion which addresses the issue being discussed.
4. **Discourse markers** which show the reader how the argument is progressing.

Instructions

INSTRUCTION AND OPERATING MANUAL
CONTENTS

Letters of complaint

COMPLAINTS

Reports

Information texts

1. There should be an address to which you are writing and your return address should be included.
2. There should be a date indicating when you wrote the letter.
3. There needs to be an appropriately formal salutation, i.e. 'Dear Sir', 'Dear Madam', 'Dear Mr Jones'.
4. There needs to be an appropriately formal ending/closing: 'Yours faithfully' (if you don't know the name of the person you have written to); 'Yours sincerely' (if you have named the person you are writing to in your opening **salutation**).

Salutation ➤ Greeting

Discourse markers ➤ Words or short phrases that indicate which direction the argument is going to develop in – for example, connectives like 'furthermore' (which indicates an extra point is being added) or 'however' (which implies that a contrary point is going to be addressed)

Find a lengthy report from a newspaper or magazine. Cut it into paragraphs. Mix up the pieces of paper and then try to rearrange the report into its original order by looking at its content and the use of discourse markers.

1. Name five types of formal writing mentioned in this module.
2. Give three features that these writing types have in common.
3. Why is there no definitive letter layout?
4. What is the purpose of the first part of a formal essay?
5. What is the thesis in an essay?

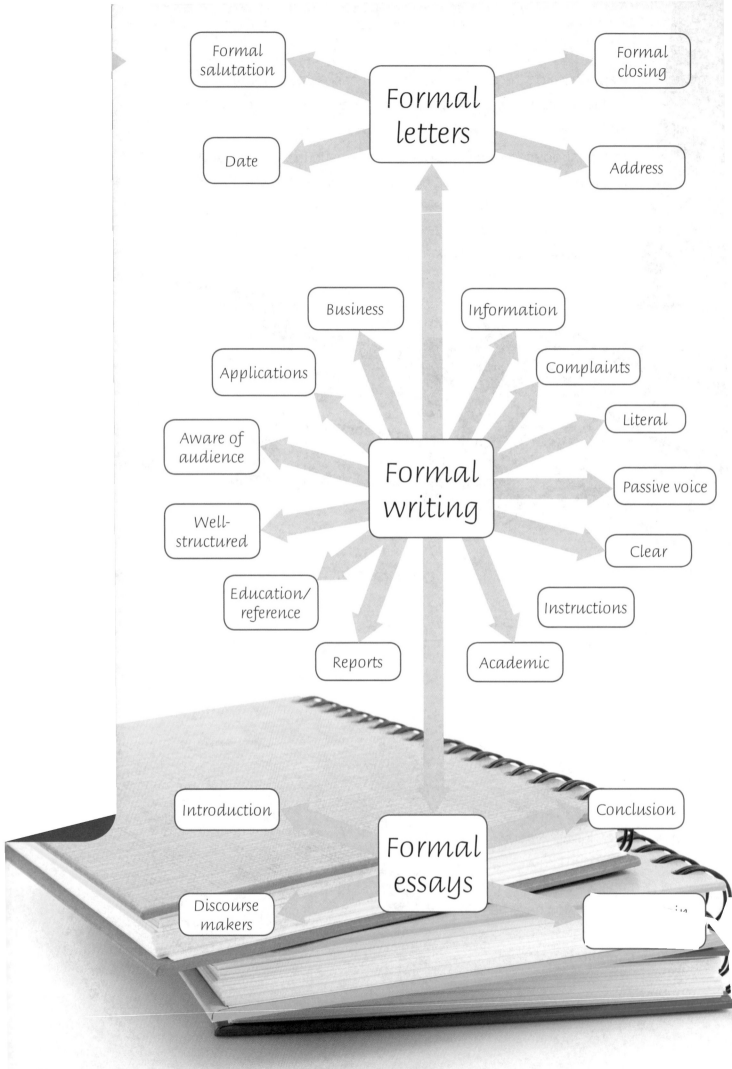

Formal letters

- Formal salutation
- Formal closing
- Date
- Address

Formal writing

- Business
- Information
- Applications
- Complaints
- Aware of audience
- Literal
- Well-structured
- Passive voice
- Education/reference
- Clear
- Reports
- Instructions
- Academic

Formal essays

- Introduction
- Conclusion
- Discourse makers

> Look at the short formal letter below. The features marked in red are incorrect or missing. In the chart below the letter are a number of statements which explain why the features in red are missing or incorrect. Some of the statements are relevant, some are not. Pick out the relevant statements and match them with the red parts of the letter. **(7)**

50 Art Street
Chicago
Illinois
?????? 1.

?????? 2.

?????? 3.

Dear Mikey babes, 4.

I wish to purchase a painting from you. I visited your exhibition at the Fulks' gallery in Chicago and was very impressed with one painting entitled 'Mars Cheese Castle'. As I understand, this was on sale for $6000. If the painting is still available and unsold, I would like to formally register my interest.

If you are willing to sell the painting, please contact me at the earliest possible opportunity. I'd love to see it hanging up in my living room; don't you think that'd be brill? 5.

Yours truly 6.

?????? 7.

Robbie Gjersoe

A	Shortened version of the recipient's address is missing.
B	The address is wrong.
C	The closing is spelled incorrectly.
D	The closing is too informal.
E	The date is missing.
F	The date is on the wrong side.
G	The postal code is missing.
H	The salutation is too informal.
I	The signature is illegible.
J	The signature is missing.
K	The style of the body text is too informal.

Before you do any kind of writing, you need to organise your ideas. You can do this in a variety of ways – and different ways suit different people with different learning styles. Here are some of the main methods and their advantages and disadvantages.

Planning in your head

➤ *Advantages* – It is quick and easy. It is fine for short responses where you do not have to write too much and the writing only needs to be organised in a simple, straightforward way.

➤ *Disadvantages* – This method is not good for longer or more complicated pieces of extended writing. It is too easy to forget things, get confused and get in a muddle. It is not easy, especially in exams, when you are writing to a time limit, to keep the plan in your head and also remember how long you need to spend on each part – and what content needs to go in each part.

Making lists

➤ *Advantages* – Making lists is a simple and straightforward process and will help you to put ideas into a logical order. Lists can easily be numbered to help with the sequence of your ideas.

➤ *Disadvantages* – If you are aiming for high grades or levels, you will be expected to make cross-references and **synthesise** your ideas. Making lists might restrict how well you link and synthesise your ideas, stopping you from achieving the highest levels or grades.

Themes
love
jealousy
injustice
power
beauty
family

Mind-maps

➤ *Advantages* – They are good for organising the sequence and development of ideas.
➤ *Disadvantages* – They can become difficult to read if too much detail is put on them. Ideally they need space to be developed well.

Spider diagrams

➤ *Advantages* – They are good for generating ideas and for working at speed.
➤ *Disadvantages* – They can get messy and difficult to read if they contain a lot of information. They will probably need to be numbered if they are going to be used to sequence ideas.

Sticky notes/ pieces of paper

Synthesise ➤
Combine ideas

➤ *Advantages* – Ideas can be moved around and re-ordered easily.

➤ *Disadvantages* – The paper can be lost, or there isn't enough room to develop ideas. How ideas are linked isn't necessarily obvious.

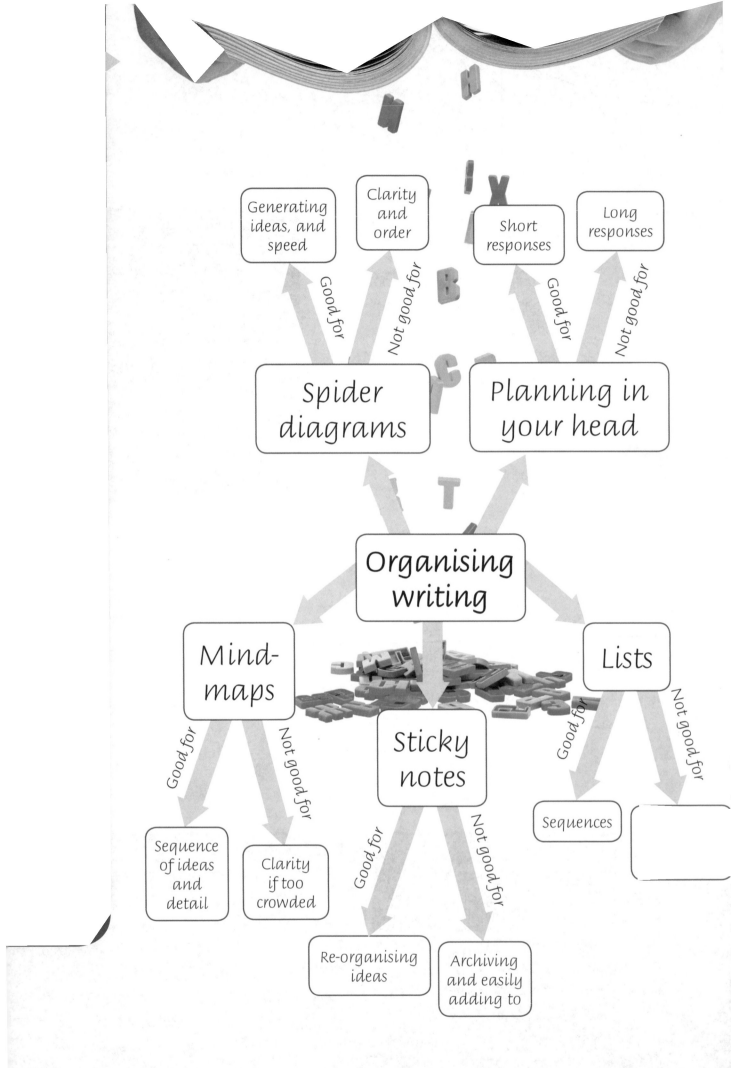

Generating ideas, and speed

Clarity and order

Short responses

Long responses

Good for

Not good for

Good for

Not good for

Spider diagrams

Planning in your head

Organising writing

Mind-maps

Lists

Sticky notes

Good for

Not good for

Good for

Not good for

Good for

Not good for

Sequence of ideas and detail

Clarity if too crowded

Sequences

Re-organising ideas

Archiving and easily adding to

Answer the questions below.

Here is a set of notes about World War I that someone has made after watching a TV documentary. They now need to write a descriptive essay about the events of World War I and they will first put the notes in chronological order (the order in which they happened), in a list.

6 April 1917 – USA declared war on Germany

7 May 1915 – The *Lusitania* was sunk by a German U-boat

28 June 1914 – Franz Ferdinand assassinated at Sarajevo

1 July 1916 – Start of the Battle of the Somme

9 November 1918 – Kaiser Wilhelm II of Germany abdicated

4 August 1914 – Britain declared war on Germany

11 November 1918 – Germany signed an armistice with the Allies – the official date of the end of World War I

29 October 1914 – Trench warfare started to dominate the Western Front

5 December 1917 – Armistice between Germany and Russia signed

1. How might each point on the list be used to write the essay? (1)

2. Why are lists likely to be better than mind-maps for organising chronological ideas? (1)

3. Why might a mind-map be a better way of planning and organising ideas if the task was to comment on the effects of the events of the war? (1)

4. What might be the advantages of using sticky notes to make a plan for this essay? (1)

5. Why would planning in the head not be a good idea for this essay? (1)

Module 10

Audiences – the 's' is important

Most texts will be written for:

➤ *a primary audience* – the main intended readers that the writer is trying to reach

➤ *secondary audiences* – anyone else who reads the text.

A writer has some control over how they influence a primary audience, but little control over how secondary audiences might read their writing, as they are often unknown.

Choosing a genre

Once you know who your primary audience is, you need to decide what the most appropriate genre would be to write in, to interest them. The primary audience will expect you to follow many of the rules of the genre that you have chosen.

When you have chosen your genre, you need to think about choosing the appropriate vocabulary for it.

The vocabulary choices will then dictate, or influence, the style and **register** that you write in.

🎧 10

Register ➤ **The level of formality of a written text**

Writing for a primary audience

Issues to consider when writing for a primary audience include:

➤ age

➤ gender

➤ class

➤ location

➤ level of education

➤ level of interest in the subject being written about.

Purpose

You also need to consider why you are writing for a particular audience. Do you want to:

Entertain? Describe? Explain?
Analyse? Comment? Review?
Advise? Inform? Persuade?
Argue? Instruct?

All of these issues will affect your choices of:

➤ language   ➤ viewpoint

➤ register   ➤ tone

➤ vocabulary ➤ sentence types.

On a big sheet of paper, write your name in the middle. Brainstorm the differences between the way you would write your life story for the following audiences and purposes:

➤ **to entertain a younger relative**

➤ **to persuade a college or university to accept you as a student.**

1. **Why is a writer's primary audience the most important?**

2. **Why is it difficult to write for secondary audiences?**

3. **What does 'register' mean and why is it important, do you think?**

4. **Give five different reasons why you might write a text.**

5. **Give four things that are affected by a writer's choice of primary audience and purpose.**

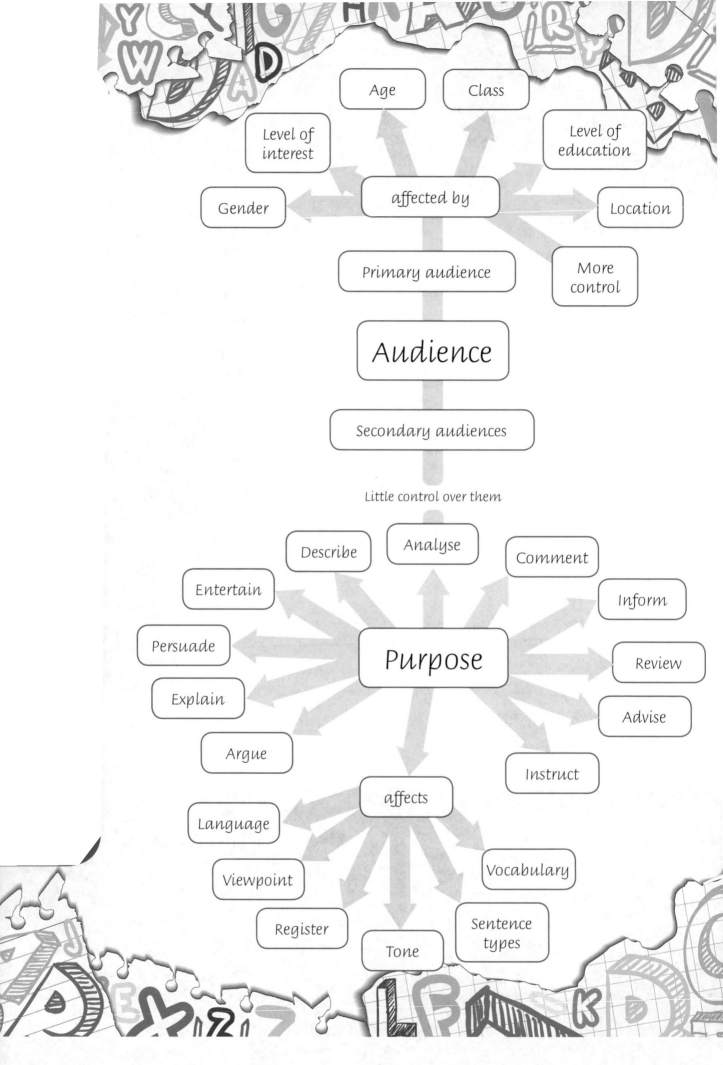

Age

Class

Level of interest

Level of education

Gender

affected by

Location

Primary audience

More control

Audience

Secondary audiences

Little control over them

Describe

Analyse

Comment

Entertain

Inform

Persuade

Purpose

Review

Explain

Advise

Argue

Instruct

affects

Language

Viewpoint

Vocabulary

Register

Sentence types

Tone

> **Answer the questions below.**

1. Which genres do these extracts mainly belong to? What is the primary purpose of all three texts? (6)

Extract 1

The truck rolled violently over on its side and tipped Idaho Smith out into the dusty ditch. Quickly, he picked himself up and glanced round to see the sprinting figures of two agents racing towards him. Quick as a flash, he rolled into the undergrowth and covered himself with as much foliage as he could muster. The figures trotted by, missing him completely – as soon as they disappeared round the next bend, Smith dusted himself down and leapt, monkey-like, over a nearby ledge and hurtled with increasing speed towards the raging torrent of the river. There was only one way to safely get away – and that involved getting wet.

Extract 2

Michelle dreamily turned and gazed towards the rugged, masculine features of the man of her dreams. The light shone from behind him, framing his dark, handsome features. She trembled with nerves – would this be the moment when…when he asked her to marry him? She adjusted her dress and took a step towards him – her heart skipped as she made her move.

Extract 3

Edvark the elf-goblin lifted his hatchet and stepped out through the door of his hut. In the distance he could hear the rumbling of the local fire-dragon and see the sparks from its latest raid falling on the tips of the mountains. It wasn't going to be a good day for this particular elf-goblin. From his grand-elf's attic he'd found a letter on parchment – ancient parchment, from before the time of the fire-dragon, telling stories of a lost place with a mysterious, dark treasure. Edvark's curiosity was going to get him in trouble one day – and that day was today.

2. Who might the primary audience be for each of the texts in this list?

    a. A school geography textbook. (1)

    b. A guide to castles in Scotland. (1)

    c. A 'How to fix your washing machine' guide. (1)

3. Match up the language features with the texts in this chart. (5)

Language features	Texts
Exaggerated, simple vocabulary	Adult novel
Short, step-by-step sentences	Child's comic book
Complex, descriptive sentences	An advert
A second-person persuasive style	An instruction manual for complex machinery
Lots of obscure specialist technical vocabulary	A quick guide to setting up a TV

Narrative and non-narrative texts – what is the difference?

Narrative texts tell some sort of story or account of events. Non-narrative texts include:

➤ cookbooks

➤ technical manuals

➤ dictionaries

➤ maps

🎧 **11**

One main difference between these types of text is how they are organised.

Non-narrative texts often have the following features:

➤ deal with cause and effect – for example, a guide on how to operate equipment, which has different sections on how different parts of the machinery affect the equipment's operation

➤ a main idea and supporting details – for example, a school textbook that explains topics or ideas

➤ alphabetical order – for example, a dictionary or encyclopaedia

➤ often, but not always, non-fiction. A **parody** guide or dictionary designed to be humorous would be non-narrative fiction.

Using several sticky notes, write down as many advantages of school uniform as you can think of. Put each advantage on a separate sticky note. Organise the sticky notes in the order that you think builds up the best argument for school uniform. Think about which ideas go together and which ideas would be best to start and end with.

Parody ➤ **An imitation of the style of a particular writer, artist or genre with deliberate exaggeration for humorous effect**

In our everyday lives, we probably read and write more non-narrative texts than any other.

Examples of everyday non-narrative texts:

➤ a shopping list
➤ a letter requesting information
➤ an e-mail requiring information about a work-related issue
➤ a technical manual
➤ an argumentative essay at school

Things to consider when writing a non-narrative text

➤ What is the best way to organise the ideas for the reader? Should it be in sections, columns, chapters, modules, etc.? Should it have headings or paragraphs?
➤ What is the purpose of the text?
➤ Is it meant to be re-read and studied as a reference guide?
➤ Is it developing an argument and discussing a range of ideas?
➤ Does it belong to a particular genre, e.g. instruction manuals, law books, computer game cheat guides?

1. What do narrative texts do?
2. Give two features of non-narrative texts.
3. Give an example of a non-narrative fiction text.
4. Give two examples of non-narrative texts that you would find in a school.
5. Give two things that you need to consider when writing a non-narrative text.

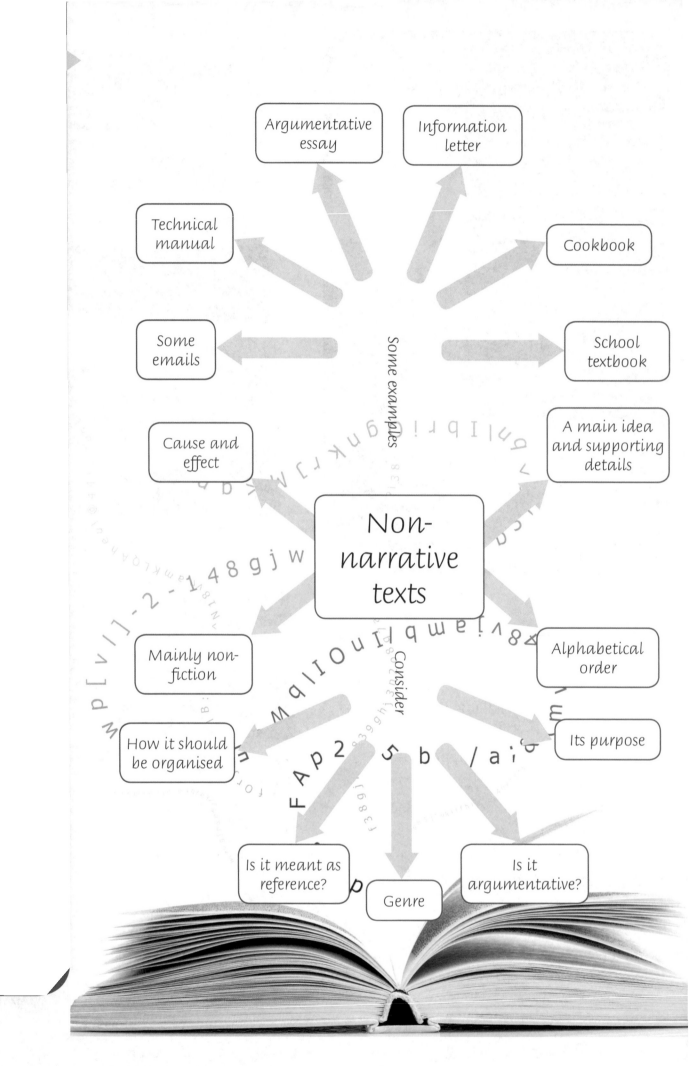

Argumentative essay

Information letter

Technical manual

Cookbook

Some emails

School textbook

Cause and effect

A main idea and supporting details

Some examples

Non-narrative texts

Mainly non-fiction

Alphabetical order

How it should be organised

Its purpose

Consider

Is it meant as reference?

Genre

Is it argumentative?

The first reason why I love folk music is that it is really easy to make with very few instruments. In the past, people had to make music with whatever they had to hand, so bones, sticks and stones were early percussion instruments. The next reason why I like folk music is that it's usually easy to play. Because it was played by ordinary working people, for their entertainment, it was often not complicated, consisting of perhaps only two or three easy-to-play chords. That means that anyone who had a little knowledge of an instrument could be a folk musician. Thirdly, the stories that are told in folk music are fascinating – and many of the songs are really just stories with a tune; classic stories with timeless storylines, of knights, battles, common folk and rich. Even if you didn't like the music of some of the songs, the stories would fascinate you. A different reason why I like folk music is that it is unfashionable at this moment in time. Who wants to follow the crowd and be the same as everyone else, mindlessly taking in what the radio and television says we are supposed to like? Not me, that's for sure. In contrast to this, I feel that folk music offers tremendous opportunities to find out about our past. Many songs have been passed down over hundreds of years and some of the 'same' songs exist in slightly different versions all over the country and indeed, all over the world. A further reason why I like folk music is that it can be enjoyed anywhere. It doesn't need expensive microphones and sound equipment (although they might sometimes help!) but it can be performed in any room, by a small number of people. Anyone who feels like joining in can add their sound to the music too. My seventh reason is a personal one – there are many performers and singers whose voices and choice of songs really appeal to me. Whether it is a distinctive female voice or a mixture of instruments making a certain sound, there are special sounds that make me feel good when I hear them. Eighth on my list of reasons is the fact that attending folk music concerts is really cheap! Because the performers don't need expensive stage sets and costumes, this means that ticket prices are kept quite low, which in turn means that fans like me can attend several concerts at a local venue for the cost of attending one big show in a massive arena. This leads on to my ninth and penultimate point, the fact that when you are at a folk music concert, you will be close to the people making the music – you will see their fingers playing their instruments and you will see the glances that musicians make to each other – the signs that they make to end the song, or to play a solo…and you won't have to look up to see it on a big video screen. Finally, I realise that folk music is not for everyone, but it does appeal to all ages and for different reasons – and hopefully will continue to do so, for several more hundreds, or even thousands, of years!

Making notes is a very important skill. Notes can be made when listening to someone speak, or from other written texts that you can re-read or review. Often, only you might need to understand the notes, but you may be making them for someone else to use, for example if you are working in a group or team and you have shared responsibilities.

How to make useful notes

Put a title and date on your notes – this will help you to remember when you made the notes and where they come in your work. If you have lots of pieces of paper to sort and organise, then this will be invaluable.

Don't limit the length of your notes as you make them – you can always sort and shorten them afterwards and this will help you to remember what you have written.

Leave spaces between your notes – this way you will be able to add extra comments and detail if you need to, later, without having to write using small handwriting.

If you have the equipment, you could record what you are listening to and make notes at a more relaxed pace later. If you do this, remember that you must usually get permission from the speaker to record them, due to reasons of politeness or **copyright**.

Keeping notes organised – paper notes

➤ Use coloured paper so that all linked notes are made on sheets of the same colour. Files with coloured dividers will do a similar job.

➤ Label and number all your pages if you use separate sheets of paper.

➤ Create an index for your notes and keep it up to date.

Copyright ➤ The legal right, given to the creator, for a fixed number of years, to print, publish, perform, film or record literary, artistic or musical material

When making notes while listening, it will probably be easier to use one colour of pen, as it will take time to swap over pens and colours – and you might miss something important. When you revisit and tidy up your notes, you then might wish to colour-code them to make them visually organised. When reading and making notes, colour-coding as you go along is a good idea.

When reading and making notes, make lists, spider diagrams or charts as you write. This will help you to organise your ideas.

Don't write everything in full – use single words or phrases wherever appropriate. Unless you are making notes for someone else, the only person who has to understand your notes is you, so if you can understand what you have written, then what you write will be fine.

Make sure you will understand the notes you have made later on. You may make notes at the start of a course, project or job and not need the information until much later.

Keeping notes organised – digitally

➤ Many smartphones have apps designed to keep notes built into their operating systems.

➤ Many free and paid apps are available designed specifically to organise notes.

➤ If using a computer, create a system of files and folders so that notes are easily accessible.

➤ Always have at least one back-up of digital files in case of hardware failure or file corruption.

➤ Back up your files regularly.

Watch and record a short (5–10 minute) TV news broadcast. While you are watching it, make notes on the broadcast, trying to include as much detail as possible. Then, watch the recorded broadcast and check it against your notes. How much did you miss and how much did you manage to include? Keep repeating this with short TV broadcasts to refine your note-making and listening skills.

1. Who might need your notes other than you?

2. Give three tips on how to make notes while listening to someone speak.

3. Give two ways of keeping paper notes organised.

4. Give two ways of keeping digital notes organised.

5. Why is digital back-up important?

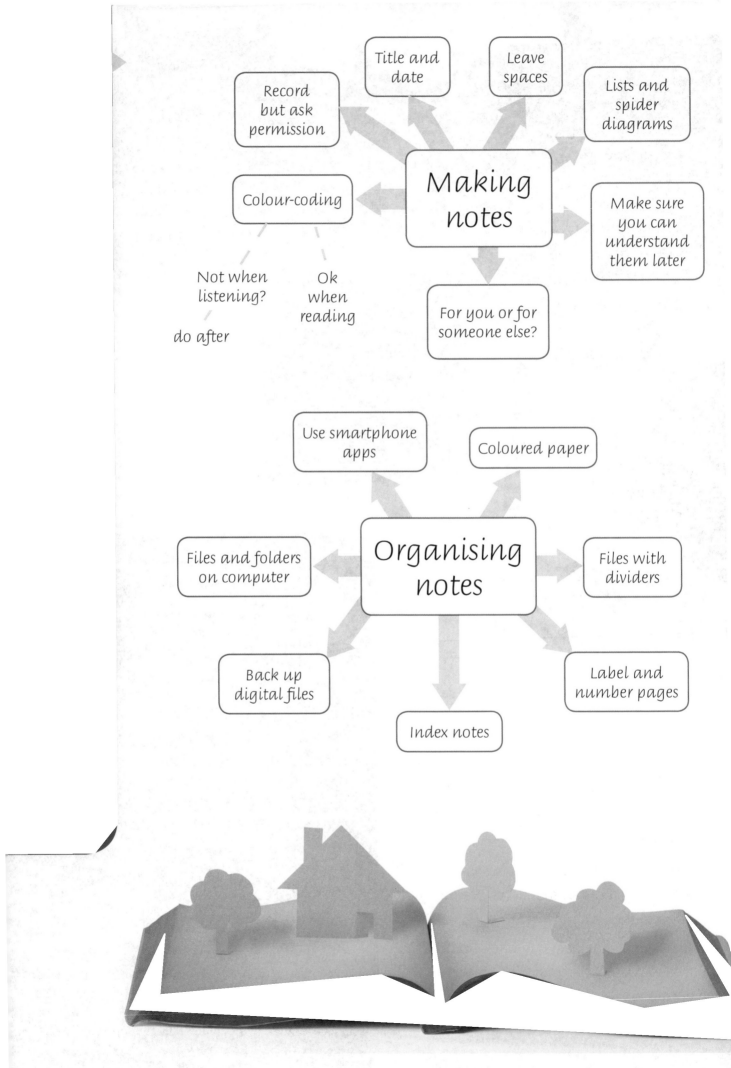

Record but ask permission

Title and date

Leave spaces

Lists and spider diagrams

Colour-coding

Making notes

Make sure you can understand them later

Not when listening?

Ok when reading

For you or for someone else?

do after

Use smartphone apps

Coloured paper

Files and folders on computer

Organising notes

Files with dividers

Back up digital files

Index notes

Label and number pages

Answer the questions below.

1. Read this passage. Use three different-coloured pens to identify the following:

    a. The key dates in the passage.   (4)

    b. The key skills that Edwina Lookup possesses.   (6)

    c. The most famous events that Edwina is connected with.   (3)

Edwina Lookup is a Derbyshire-based lady, who is primarily known for her music photography. She was born in 1979 in Cromford, where she attended the local school. She left school in 1997 after doing A levels and immediately set about combining her interest in photography with her wide-ranging interests in music. Edwina developed a photographic style which involved great compositional skills and awareness of colour. Not satisfied with achieving national exposure for her photography in the monthly photo magazine 'Photography International', in 2004 Edwina also began a music career of her own. Having developed good kinaesthetic skills in handling a camera, Edwina found it easy to take up her childhood instrument of the fiddle. She formed a duo with school friend Doris Gabb and the two of them started playing local folk clubs. In the duo, Edwina sang and played the fiddle. In 2008, Edwina and Doris won a National Youth Music competition and were chosen by an advertising agency to be the face of a 'Pongofoot Trainer Insoles' campaign, thus allowing Edwina to add 'fashion model' to her list of achievements.

2. Now read the passage below. Identify what you think are the key facts. Summarise the passage in full sentences, in half the number of words, without missing out any key facts.   (5)

Based in Queens, New York, The Ramones formed in 1974. Originally, the band was a trio consisting of Joey Ramone (vocals, drums; born Jeffrey Hyman, May 19, 1951), Johnny Ramone (guitar; born John Cummings, Oct. 8, 1951) and Dee Dee Ramone (bass; born Douglas Colvin, Sept. 18, 1951), but expanded to a four-person line-up with the addition of Tommy Ramone (born Tom Erdelyi, Jan. 29, 1952), who later became the group's manager. The group's members took the last name 'Ramone' and dressed in ripped jeans and black leather jackets, as a tribute to '50s rockers. The group played their first concert on March 30, 1974. Two months after the show, Joey became the vocalist and Tommy became the band's drummer. For the next year, they played regularly at a nightclub called CBGBs, earning a dedicated cult following. All of The Ramones sets clocked in at about 20 minutes, featuring short, two-minute songs. By the end of 1975, The Ramones had secured a recording contract with Sire; they were the first New York punk band to sign a contract. Early in 1976, The Ramones recorded their debut album for about $6,000. This album, simply called 'Ramones', was released in the spring and managed to climb to 111 on the U.S. album charts. On July 4, the band made their first appearance in Britain, where their records were becoming a big influence on a new generation of bands. (236 words)

Creating effective openings

To create an effective opening, a writer must have a clear sense of the **audience** that is being written for and the **purpose** of the writing.

Example 1 – Using adjectives, adverbs, rhetorical questions and complex sentences in a descriptive opening

He gazed longingly at her soft, wavy hair as it was being blown gently by the coastal breeze.

She stared thoughtfully out to sea, beyond the pier, beyond the waves pattering gently on the beach below, completely unaware of his presence.

He wanted to say something to her – but could he?

Purpose – to intrigue and create interest
Audience – teenagers or older

Descriptive openings

If you are writing the opening of a novel or story, you would want to get the reader's attention, to make them carry on reading. Depending on the age and interests of the reader, you would use different techniques to make them interested.

Instructional middles

If you are writing the middle of a set of instructions, you would want to make the purpose of the instructions clear. You would use vocabulary that is suitable for the kind of person who wants to follow the instructions.

13

Ellipsis ➤ The omission of a word or words that are not needed, or able to be understood from clues in the surrounding writing

Imperatives ➤ Command words

Creating effective endings

To create an effective ending, it is again important to think about the **audience** and the **purpose** of the writing.

Descriptive or story endings

These can be quite varied, but to write an effective ending you need to ask yourself some questions. Do I want to reveal everything? Do I want to leave some things to the imagination of the reader? Will there be a sequel? Do I want to shock, surprise or cause other feelings?

Example 2 – Using short sentences, imperatives, a personal tone and technical vocabulary in instructional writing

> By following this section, you will quickly be able to use the advanced features on your new camera.
>
> Find the button marked 'Stabiliser' and ensure that it is set to the 'Off' setting. Then insert the camera battery in the battery compartment. The battery compartment is made of red plastic and is on the bottom of the camera.

Purpose – instructional writing
Audience – all ages, but assuming some basic knowledge of cameras

Example 3 – Using ellipsis, adjectives and varied sentences in a descriptive ending

> She stopped. She turned. It all came flooding back now – why hadn't she realised before? There was only one thing to do and that was to go back again to the dark, sad house...

Purpose – to entertain and conclude, but leave some things to the reader's imagination
Audience – teenagers or older

The End

Write these three story openings on three separate pieces of paper.

1. He walked through the door – his handsome, chiselled features were silhouetted moodily against the light.

2. He walked threateningly through the door and his angry features were carved out against the harsh moonlight.

3. He bounced through the door. His humorous features were exaggerated by the glowing light.

On three further pieces of paper, write endings to each one in the same style. Swap them around, matching different starts and endings. What new effects would this create? Would they all work? How might the different endings change what happens in the middle?

1. According to the example in this module, what might be the purpose of the opening of a romantic novel?

2. Give an example of an adjective and an adverb from Example 1.

3. Give an example of an imperative from Example 2.

4. Give an example of ellipsis from Example 3.

5. What is one question you might ask yourself when writing a story ending?

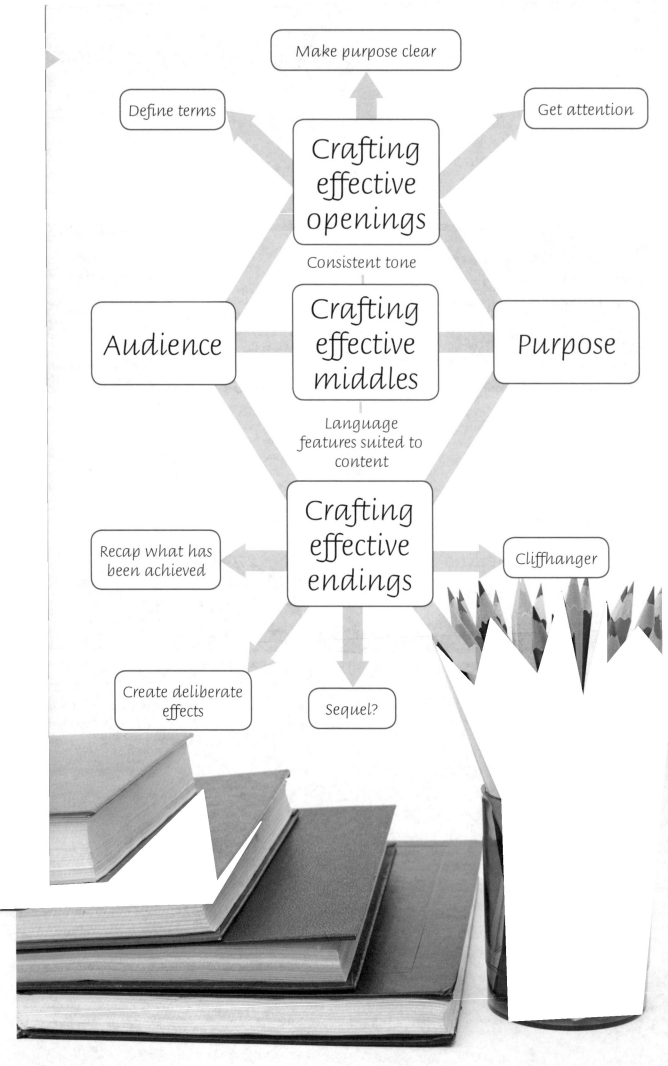

Make purpose clear

Define terms

Get attention

Crafting effective openings

Consistent tone

Audience

Crafting effective middles

Purpose

Language features suited to content

Recap what has been achieved

Crafting effective endings

Cliffhanger

Create deliberate effects

Sequel?

Answer the questions below.

1. Creating effective openings

   a. Write the opening paragraph of an adventure story for teenagers or older, using adjectives, adverbs, alliteration and a variety of sentences for effect. (5)

   b. Write the opening of a letter to a friend, inviting them to spend a day out with you and your family, using informal vocabulary, a variety of sentence types, exaggeration and a rhetorical question. (5)

   c. Write the opening of a set of instructions for a new phone, using imperatives, short sentences and technical vocabulary. (5)

   d. Write the opening of a formal letter asking permission for a child to have a day off school to go on holiday, using an appropriate style, respectful vocabulary and complex sentences. (4)

2. Creating an effective middle

   Read the passage below – in each case, choose the best word from each of the three choices, in order to create an overall **formal** tone. (5)

   The main reason why the Anglo-Saxons **nicked/stuffed/buried** treasure was, we believe, to keep it safe from raiders. **Brain-boxes/experts/clever-clogs** are still debating the significance of the treasure **swag/hoard/boodle** found in Staffordshire, but it may never reveal its secrets. One expert was **rumoured/ parroted/quoted** as saying that recent discoveries have made us change completely the way that we view the **ancient/past-it/decrepit** world and that many of our history books will need to be re-written.

3. Creating effective endings

   a. Write the final paragraph to a mystery story, without giving away what happened, but dropping hints through the description and punctuation. (4)

   b. Write the ending of a letter, in which you have complained about the treatment you received at a famous theme park when you lost your glasses on one of the rides. (2)

   c. Write the final part of the instructions for a new games console, assuming that the person reading has never played or used one before. (2)

   d. Write the ending of a letter to a friend, in which you have tried to persuade them to do a dangerous sports activity. (2)

Planning and organising

The first stage in creating a piece of work is to plan it – nobody gets things right first time and having an outline will help you when you come to do a rough full draft. See Module 9 'Organising writing' for more details on organising your ideas.

Drafting

After you have planned your ideas, you then need to do a rough draft. There are different ways you might do this.

Method 1 – Writing your ideas out all in one go and then changing them afterwards

Advantages:

➤ The writer quickly gets an overall idea of how the final work might look.

➤ Less chance of suffering from writer's block.

Disadvantages:

➤ There is a tendency to rush and the draft might lack essential detail.

➤ Has to be re-read several times.

Method 2 – Writing your ideas out and changing them as you go along

Advantages:

➤ More focus on the detail of each sentence.

➤ Further ideas develop from the conscious crafting of individual words and sentences.

Disadvantages:

➤ Might seem slower than Method 1.

➤ More difficult to have an overview of the whole text until it is nearly finished.

Homophones ➤ Words that sound the same but have different spellings and meanings

Editing

Drafting and editing are interconnected and happen simultaneously, but after a good rough draft has been written, a final editing process is needed. This is to make sure:

1. The text is of a consistent standard throughout – are the style, tone and register always as they should be? Are the choices of vocabulary and sentences of a consistent quality throughout?
2. The whole piece of writing is balanced – are some sections over-long, or too short?

Proofreading

This is the final stage of checking small details before the work is completed. When proofreading, you need to:

➤ Check for mistakes at word or sentence level.

➤ Look for mistakes of extra words added in or words missed out.

➤ Look for common errors, e.g. its/it's.

➤ If work has been done on the computer, make sure that a dictionary has been used alongside the spellcheck to ensure that the correct words have been chosen, especially with **homophones**.

Get a piece of fully drafted school work. Make a photocopy of it. Give the photocopied copy to a friend or relative and get them to check and correct it. You do the same with the original. Compare the two versions and see how many mistakes and corrections two people identify, as opposed to one.

1. Give two ways you might draft a piece of work.
2. What is a question you might ask yourself when editing work?
3. What is one thing that you need to be careful of when proofreading work done on the computer?
4. What is one common error mentioned in this module that you might proofread for?
5. Why will homophones not usually be flagged up as wrong by computer software?

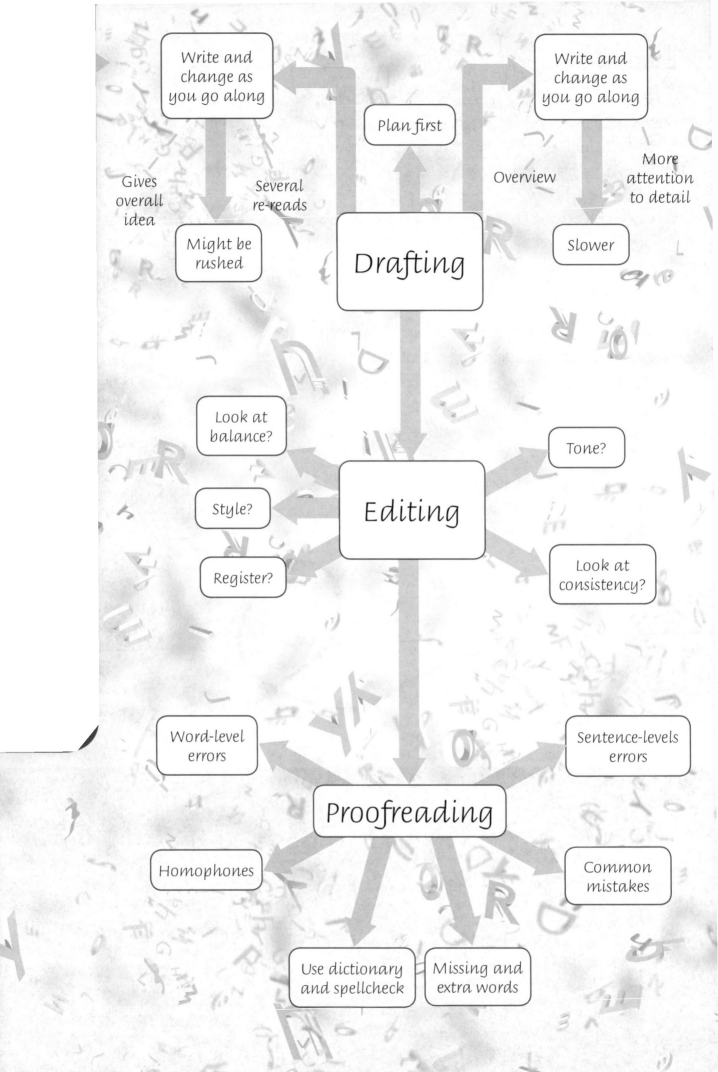

Write and change as you go along

Plan first

Write and change as you go along

Gives overall idea

Several re-reads

Overview

More attention to detail

Might be rushed

Slower

Drafting

Look at balance?

Tone?

Style?

Editing

Register?

Look at consistency?

Word-level errors

Sentence-levels errors

Proofreading

Homophones

Common mistakes

Use dictionary and spellcheck

Missing and extra words

Answer the questions below.

1. This passage is a draft of a personal statement. It was written by a student who is hoping to use it to apply for university. A number of errors have been spotted while proofreading and they have been highlighted by the writer. Re-write the passage so that the errors are corrected. (14)

> Since visiting Haworth in West Yorkshire, I have been **intrigud** by the Brontë Sisters, which has further **lead** to a passion for English literature in **general experiencing** the inspirational **senery** for the various novels has caused me to revel in finding links between writers and their texts, as well as finding a personal connection with a novel and the writer. I find **wuthering heights** in particular a captivating novel, which I have **enthusiastcally** studied at A-level. However, my favourite novel would have to be *To Kill a Mockingbird*, by Harper Lee, which I found to be sensationally thought-provoking. For me**;** what makes English Literature such an inspiring and appealing subject to study is not just the impact that books leave on a person, but the varying opinions and alternative interpretations that spring from reading them. I have a **desiree** to develop and expand my knowledge of **literature** genres, key literary movements and the techniques used by writers to communicate a message or meaning. In class, I actively contribute to discussions and debates, as well as **had** a fascination with the purposes and personal aims of writers. Being on the college Student Council has further improved my confidence when talking to **unfammiliar** people and I have been able to **voicing** my opinion, without causing conflict.

   a. What impression would sending in an uncorrected draft like this create? (1)

   b. Do you think the student's application for a place on an English course would be successful? Why? (2)

2. Here is another passage in which the writer makes lots of common homophone errors. Spot the errors. (10)

> While I was living inn Stoke-on-Trent, their were many things that I liked. Wan thing that I liked was the food. Oatcakes are a speciality of the area and lots of people eat them every day. Ewe can by them from oatcake shops which ewe don't get anywhere else in the country. It's a shame that they are knot available anywhere else in Briton, as I am shore that many people wood like them.

Learning spellings

There are several ways to try and learn spellings. Here are some techniques you might want to try:

> Create a spelling log – make a list of words you find difficult to remember.

> Every time you use a word you haven't used before, check it in a dictionary.

> Use 'Spell-speak' – say words the way they are spelled, rather than how they are usually pronounced, e.g. Wed-nes-day – Wednesday; rasp-berry – raspberry.

Wed-nes-day

> Find words within words, e.g. justice – just-ice.

> Count the syllables in words.

> Invent and use **mnemonics**, e.g. **N**ot **E**very **C**at **E**ats **S**quidgy **S**ausages **A**nd **R**ice **Y**et (Necessary).

> Learn the root word, e.g. international, internal, interview (inter = between).

> Learn spelling rules. Keep lists of them in a spelling log.

Mnemonic ➤

A pattern of letters, ideas or associations which assists in remembering something

- 'q' is always written as 'qu'.
- If a word ends in a consonant plus 'y', change the 'y' to 'i', before adding any ending, e.g. country – countries. If a word ends in a vowel plus 'y' just add 's', e.g. monkey – monkeys.
- When 'c' is followed by 'e', 'i' or 'y', it sounds like 's'. Otherwise it sounds like 'k':
  - 's' sound: centre, ceiling, circle, cycle
  - 'k' sound: cottage, cave, cream, curious, clever.

- 'ti', 'ci', 'si' are three pairs of letters used to say 'sh', e.g. station, decision, intermission.

Some common spelling rules you might wish to learn

- If a word of more than one syllable ends in a 't', preceded by a single vowel, and has the stress on the last syllable, double the final consonant, e.g. permit – permitted / admit – admitted / regret – regretted. However, do not double the final 't' in words like visit – visited / benefit – benefited.

- Most words that end in the letter 'f' become plural by adding the suffix 'ves'. However, there are a few words that don't fit this rule, such as 'chiefs' and 'roofs'.

- 'i' comes before 'e' when it is pronounced 'ee', except when it follows 'c':
  - Sounds like 'ee' but not after 'c': brief, field, priest
  - After 'c': receive, deceive, ceiling.
- 'e' comes before 'i' when it sounds like 'ay' as in 'neighbour' and 'weigh'.

Get a notebook and write each spelling rule in this module on separate pages. As you read at school and at home, add examples of words that match each rule, to build up a spelling log.

1. **Give three different ways of learning spellings.**
2. **What is the rule for words ending in a consonant plus 'y'?**
3. **When 'c' is followed by 'e', 'i' or 'y', what sound does it make?**
4. **'ti', 'ci', 'si' can be used to make which sound?**
5. **Most words that end in the letter 'f' become plural by adding which suffix?**

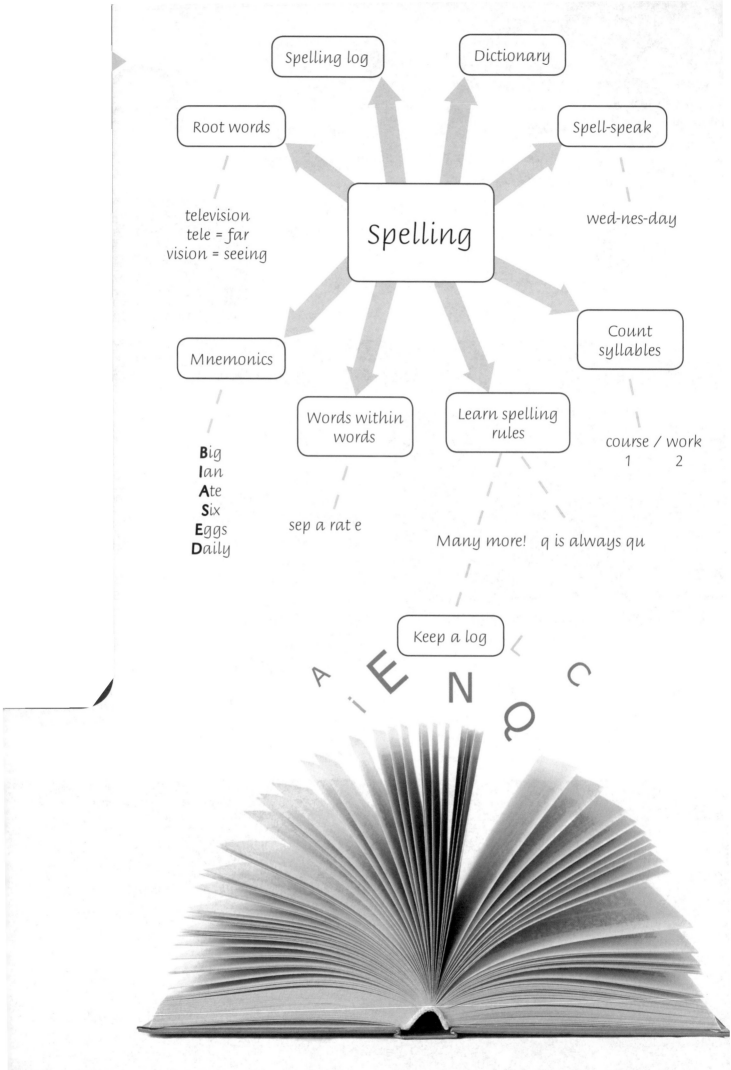

Spelling log

Dictionary

Root words

Spell-speak

television
tele = far
vision = seeing

Spelling

wed-nes-day

Mnemonics

Count
syllables

Words within
words

Learn spelling
rules

course / work
1   2

Big
Ian
Ate
Six
Eggs
Daily

sep a rat e

Many more!   q is always qu

Keep a log

Answer the questions below.

1. In the following exercise only one spelling in each group of three is correct. Identify the correct spelling in each group.

    a. Rasspberry / Raspberry / Razberry   (1)

    b. Februay / Februery / February   (1)

    c. Necessity / Neccessity / Neccessaty   (1)

    d. Libary / Librery / Library   (1)

    e. Naybor / Neighbour / Nieghbour

    f. Rumour / Rumer / Roomor

    g. Adrress / Address / Adress

    h. Dissappoint / Disappoint / Disapoint

    i. Greatful / Greitful / Grateful

    j. Hypocrissy / Hypocrisy / Hypocrassy

2. Put the correct ending on these underlined words that end in a vowel/single 'l' to make the sentences make sense.

Example – I <u>travel</u> to Egypt on a plane. Answer – I travelled to Egypt on a plane.

    a. The food was <u>appal</u>.   (1)

    b. I am going <u>travel</u> before I go to university.   (1)

    c. Michelle decided to dress <u>formal</u> for the ball.   (1)

    d. I <u>usual</u> shop here.   (1)

    e. "Do you live <u>local</u>?"   (1)

3. Put the correct ending on these underlined words that end in a 't' to make these sentences make sense.

Example – I was not <u>permit</u> to play football. Answer – I was not permitted to play football.

    a. I <u>admit</u> my guilt to the court yesterday.   (1)

    b. Sheila <u>regret</u> her actions.   (1)

    c. I <u>benefit</u> from last week's exercise.   (1)

    d. I <u>visit</u> my relations last month.   (1)

    e. I have <u>commit</u> no crime.   (1)

4. Unscramble the words underlined in these sentences – they all contain a ti/ci/si type 'sh' sound.

    a. The man was waiting at the <u>oatnits</u>.   (1)

    b. Everyone sang the <u>lanainot</u> anthem.   (1)

    c. "Don't waste my <u>riceopus</u> time!"   (1)

    d. <u>Sessionops</u> is nine-tenths of the law.   (1)

    e. The class didn't understand <u>franticso</u> in their Maths lesson.   (1)

By the end of KS3 you will be expected to be familiar with less common punctuation marks such as semi-colons and colons.

Semi-colons

1. A semi-colon [;] marks a long gap or pause in a sentence.
2. In terms of the length of pause, it is sometimes described as being between a comma and a colon.
3. Semi-colons are used between **clauses** which could exist on their own, but which are closely related or linked.

> **Clause ➤**
> **A group of related words containing a subject and a verb**

4. Semi-colons are used to separate complex lists.

Four men were in line for the prize: the previous winner; the young upstart; the old-stager and the whizz-kid favourite.

5. A semi-colon is used when a second clause adds information to or explains the first clause.

Nobody said anything; they knew who the winner was going to be.

> ✋ Read three pages of a newspaper or magazine and highlight every semi-colon and colon that you find. For each one, work out the reason it is being used.

He couldn't do the exam; he had forgotten his pen.

She was happy; her new dress had arrived.

Colons

1. A colon [:] indicates a long pause in a sentence.

2. It is longer than a semi-colon, but not as long as a full-stop.

3. A colon can introduce a list:

   The camera had many advantages: a viewfinder, dust removal, two free lenses and a flash.

4. It separates clauses which could be separate sentences, but which are linked by their meanings:

   I like coffee: my sister prefers tea.

5. A colon can be used before a quotation or speech:

   The King spoke: "Now is the time that we must all pull together."

6. It can also be used before clauses which explain the first statement:

   The manager was well thought of: he looked after people, complimented them often and bought them presents when they did well.

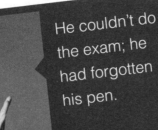

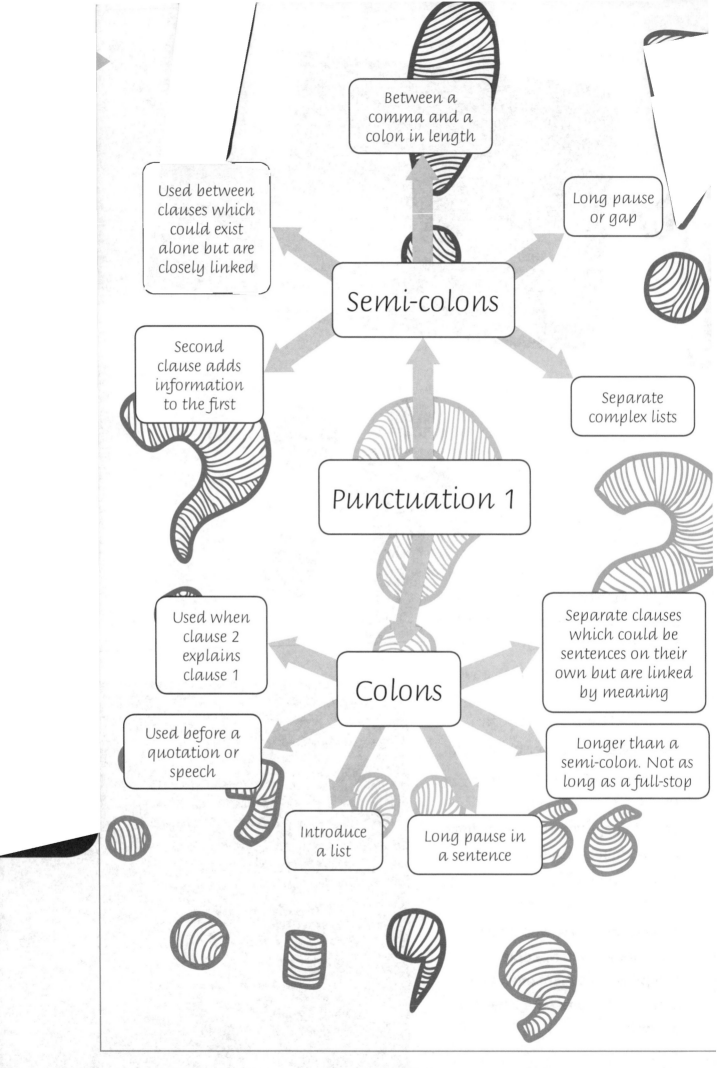

Between a comma and a colon in length

Used between clauses which could exist alone but are closely linked

Long pause or gap

Second clause adds information to the first

Semi-colons

Separate complex lists

Punctuation 1

Used when clause 2 explains clause 1

Separate clauses which could be sentences on their own but are linked by meaning

Colons

Used before a quotation or speech

Longer than a semi-colon. Not as long as a full-stop

Introduce a list

Long pause in a sentence

Semi-colons

1. Put the semi-colons in the correct place in these sentences.

    a. I am going home I will set out from there. (1)

    b. It rained heavily we still went for our walk. (1)

    c. It was too dark we couldn't finish the trip. (1)

    d. I am going home moreover, I will set out from there. (1)

    e. It rained heavily however, we still went for our walk. (1)

    f. It was too rich we couldn't eat it. (1)

    g. We finished the exercise the test was over. (1)

    h. There were many different people: the enthusiastic youngsters the veteran performers the weekend amateurs all were taking part. (1)

2. Write ten sentences of your own which use semi-colons correctly. (10)

Colons

3. Put the colons in the correct place in these sentences.

    a. There were only two things that Fred worried about where the colon went and why it was used. (1)

    b. He only needed one thing to get through the week money. (1)

    c. Rule number one the teacher is always right. (1)

    e. Everything went right on that day they won the lottery; the electricity came back on; Jane got a new job and their pet dog was found. (1)

    f. The teacher spoke "Pens down and pay attention to what I am going to say." (1)

    g. I enjoy reading novels by Jane Austen are among my favourites. (1)

    h. There is only one thing left to do now confess while you still have time. (1)

    i. You are left with only one option keep going until you have got it right. (1)

4. Write ten sentences of your own which use colons correctly. (10)

Apostrophes of omission

Apostrophes of **omission** are used to replace missed-out letters. Letters are often missed out when people are talking and words are shortened. They are used more in informal writing – in formal writing they can give the impression of informality.

Examples

Cannot – gets shortened to can't

In this example, the apostrophe stands for the missed-out letters taken from 'cannot' (cannot). The apostrophe is placed where those letters previously were. This rule usually applies, as shown below:

don't

can't

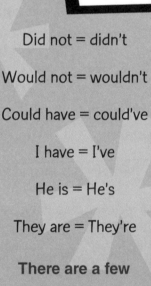

Did not = didn't

Would not = wouldn't

Could have = could've

I have = I've

He is = He's

They are = They're

There are a few exceptions:

Will not = won't

O'clock = this stands for the old-fashioned saying 'of the clock'

Omission ➤ Leaving something out

 17

Possession ➤ Belonging

Apostrophes of **possession** are used to show when one thing belongs to another.

Rule 1

If a word does not end in 's', add 's to show possession.

Dave's book = The book belonging to Dave (Dave ends in 'e' so add 's)

Hannah's work = The work belonging to Hannah (Hannah ends in 'h' so add 's)

Rule 2

If a word does end in 's', put the apostrophe after the 's' to show possession.

James' book = The book belonging to James (James ends in 's', so put the apostrophe after the 's')

The girls' team = The team belonging to the girls – plural – several girls ('girls' ends in 's' so put the apostrophe after the 's')

Go through two pages of a magazine and find as many apostrophes of possession and omission as possible. Collect these examples and make two posters, entitled 'Apostrophes of possession' and 'Apostrophes of omission'.

1. What does 'omission' mean?
2. What does 'possession' mean?
3. What does the apostrophe stand for in 'can't'?
4. In the phrase 'The boy's team', how many boys are being referred to?
5. In the phrase 'The boys' team', how many boys are being referred to?

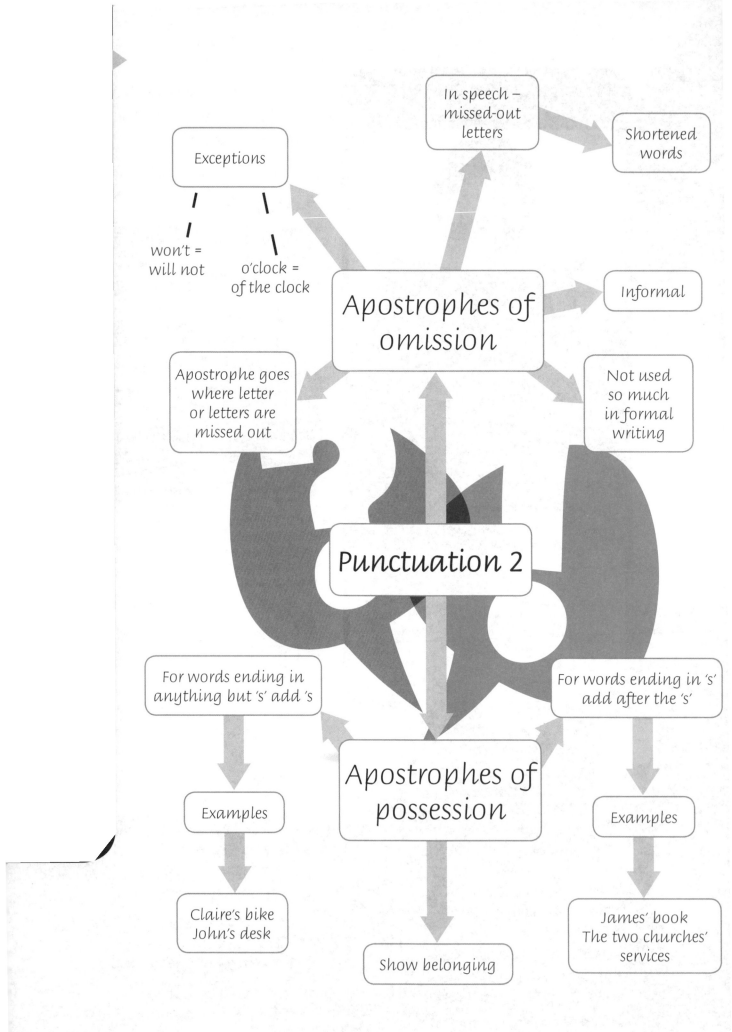

In speech –
missed-out
letters

Shortened
words

Exceptions

won't =
will not

o'clock =
of the clock

Apostrophes of
omission

Informal

Apostrophe goes
where letter
or letters are
missed out

Not used
so much
in formal
writing

Punctuation 2

For words ending in
anything but 's' add 's

For words ending in 's'
add after the 's'

Apostrophes of
possession

Examples

Examples

Claire's bike
John's desk

James' book
The two churches'
services

Show belonging

Apostrophes of omission

1. Put the apostrophes of omission into these sentences.

    a. Saffron couldnt believe that she had got the question wrong. (1)

    b. Dean hadnt done his homework. (1)

    c. Kayleigh shouldnt have eaten all the cakes. (1)

    d. "Ive got it!" shouted Ryan. (1)

    e. "Wheres the exit?" asked Abigail. (1)

    f. Kim didnt understand what she had been asked to do. (1)

    g. "I couldve done that!" remarked Mr Rashid. (1)

    h. Joe shouldve been smarter when he went for his interview. (1)

    i. "Whered Jake go?" asked Jack. (1)

    j. "Lucy wont do the reading," explained Miss Sowter. (1)

2. Write ten sentences of your own that use apostrophes of omission correctly. (10)

Apostrophes of possession

3. Put the apostrophes of possession in the correct places in these sentences.

    a. Joes Pub is in New York. (1)

    b. Nobody understood why Olivers answer was wrong. (1)

    c. Lukes bag had broken. (1)

    d. Matthew was distracted by Lauras chatter. (1)

    e. Poppys pen had been taken by Sadie. (1)

    f. Syed and Charlies work was better than expected. (1)

    g. James excuse for not doing his homework wasn't accepted by the
       teacher. (1)

    h. Lots of girls teams took part in the tournament. (1)

    i. The girls bag was returned to her. (1)

    j. Frances grade was the best in the class. (1)

4. Write ten sentences of your own that use apostrophes of possession correctly. (10)

Sentence parts

Within sentences there are a number of parts. The main part of a sentence is called the main clause. Other clauses are called **subordinate clauses**.

> **Subordinate clause ➤**
> A part of a sentence that doesn't make sense on its own – it depends on the main clause for its meaning

In the second version, by leaving the main clause until the end of the sentence, greater tension is created, because the reader doesn't know what the main reason for the sentence is straight away.

Here is an example of a sentence with a main clause and a subordinate clause:

Jim played the guitar, *because he was in a band.*

⇧　　　　　　　　　⇧

Main clause　　　　*Subordinate clause*

If you change the order of the main clause and the subordinate clause, you can create a different emphasis in the sentence:

Because he was in a band, **Jim played the guitar.**

⇧　　　　　　　　　⇧

Subordinate clause　　　**Main clause**

Sentences with more than two clauses

Many sentences have more than two clauses. These sentences can be arranged in a variety of ways, with different types of emphasis. Look at these examples:

Bill played the mandolin, *despite his age*, <u>because he enjoyed it</u>.

⬆ **Main clause**   ⬆ *Subordinate clause 1*   ⬆ <u>Subordinate clause 2</u>

Despite his age, **Bill played the mandolin,** <u>because he enjoyed it.</u>

⬆ *Subordinate clause 1*   ⬆ **Main clause**   ⬆ <u>Subordinate clause 2</u>

<u>Because he enjoyed it,</u> **Bill played the mandolin,** *despite his age.*

⬆ <u>Subordinate clause 2</u>   ⬆ **Main clause**   ⬆ *Subordinate clause 1*

When writing, therefore, it is best to try different variations of the same sentence, in order to see which works best. When you write, consider which part of the sentence you want to emphasise, or whether you want to build up tension, or create surprise.

Find a sentence from a book, magazine or newspaper that contains two clauses. Write each clause on a separate sticky note or piece of paper. Change the order of the sentence around to see if it still makes sense and to see how the emphasis is changed. When changing the sentence order around, do you have to add or change any words slightly?

1. What is a main clause?
2. What is a subordinate clause?
3. What happens to the emphasis in a sentence if you swap the order of the main and subordinate clauses?
4. If you have a sentence with a main clause and two subordinate clauses, how many different ways has this module shown you that it can be rearranged?
5. What should you consider when you are choosing sentence order?

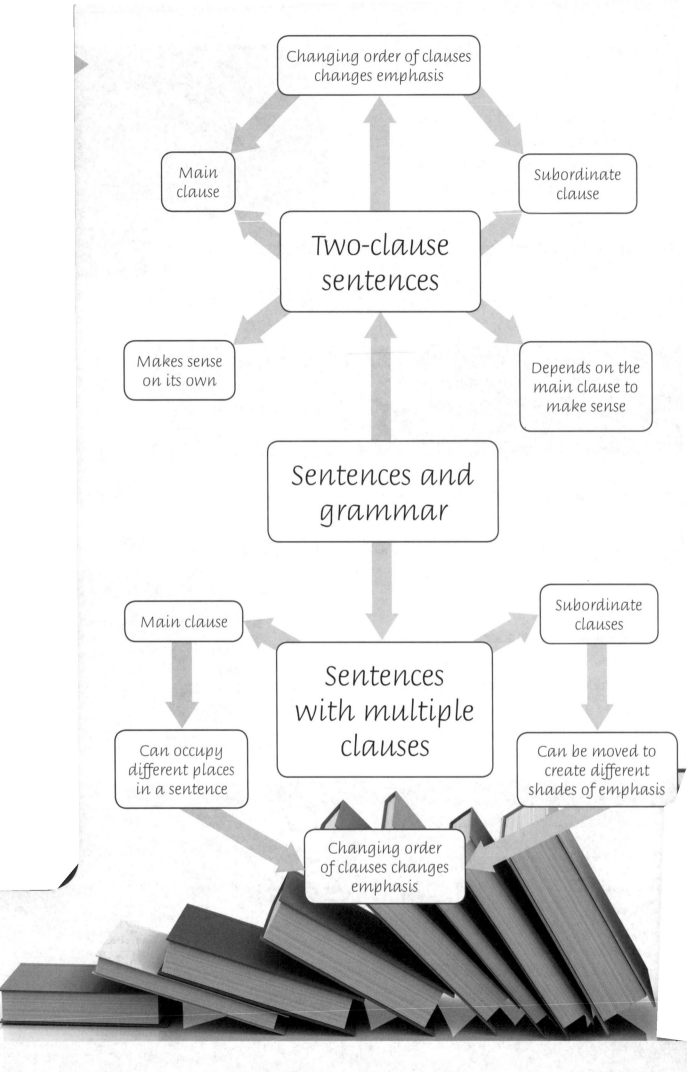

Changing order of clauses changes emphasis

Main clause

Subordinate clause

Two-clause sentences

Makes sense on its own

Depends on the main clause to make sense

Sentences and grammar

Main clause

Subordinate clauses

Sentences with multiple clauses

Can occupy different places in a sentence

Can be moved to create different shades of emphasis

Changing order of clauses changes emphasis

1. Identify the main clause and the subordinate clause in each of these sentences.

   a. Becky didn't do her homework, because she had lost her book. (2)

   b. Sadie said that she understood the work, which was unusual for her. (2)

   c. Jake put his head on the desk, because he was tired. (2)

   d. Despite being a well-behaved boy, Alex was moved by the teacher. (2)

   e. Although she had been away, Laura got top marks in the exam. (2)

   f. Sara laughed, because Sophie dropped her sweets. (2)

   g. Emily's work was good, despite her being untidy. (2)

   h. Although he was Head boy, Jack was a disruptive influence. (2)

   i. Tyler revised thoroughly, because he wanted to succeed. (2)

   j. Because she had a cold, Courtney was absent. (2)

2. Re-write all of these sentences with the order of the main clause and the subordinate clause reversed. (20)

Sentences with more than two clauses

3. Identify the main clause and the subordinate clauses in each of these sentences.

   a. Although he was very young, Grant was a great musician, who many people admired. (3)

   b. Mike loved painting, because it gave him an extra income, despite his teaching job. (3)

   c. Although his children didn't like it, Gerald's beard grew, because he didn't shave it. (3)

   d. Robbie wrote down all his ideas, although they were only rough, because he liked to draft his work. (3)

   e. Donna, although she was a married woman, worked away from her family. (3)

   f. Preston, despite being the name of a place, was also a boy's name. (3)

   g. Chicago, one of the largest cities in America, was home to the Fulks family. (3)

   h. Tara and Rob, parents of Clayton, managed to pay for his education. (3)

   i. Despite the cold weather, Ed went to work, but got stuck on the way there. (3)

   j. Whenever they sang together, despite not liking each other, the couple had success. (3)

4. Re-write the sentences above, but put the clauses in a different order. There are several possible ways of doing this for each sentence. (10)

Sentence length for effect

Different types of sentences can be used to create different effects. There are no hard-and-fast rules for what is right or wrong when using sentence lengths, but there are some good general ways that you might create different sentences for different purposes.

Short sentences can be used:

➤ *To create impact* – e.g. Really?

➤ *As part of speech*, e.g. When shouting – e.g. "Stop it! Now!"

➤ *To make a point* – e.g. That *is* the answer.

➤ *To create suspense or tension* – e.g. They walked slowly. The door was shut. No sounds were heard.

➤ *To write instructions or give commands* – e.g. Open the box. Take the money. Spend it wisely.

➤ *To make your ideas clearer* – e.g. The gears rotate. They then power the engine.

➤ *To create the impression that someone is not very clever* – e.g. Yeah. Right. OK.

Pompous ➤ When someone acts or sounds as if they are more important than they actually are

Subject ➤ What a sentence is about – all grammatically correct sentences should have a subject

Note how in some of these examples, the rule about a sentence needing a **subject** and a verb is sometimes broken for deliberate effect.

🎧 19

Longer sentences can be used:

➤ **To create descriptive detail** – e.g. The scratched door, harmed by the claws of the vicious dogs inside, swung squeakily on its rusty, ancient hinges. Vince pushed gingerly at its wooden surface and stepped nervously – like someone who had never done this before – into the dark, sullen interior, wondering what secrets he would uncover.

➤ **To add extra information** – e.g. Before you cook the steak, ensure that the oven has been heated to the right temperature, so that the steak spends the correct amount of time in the oven at the required temperature.

➤ **To create tension or suspense** – e.g. There, high on the hill, surrounded by trees and rarely visited by humankind, stood the house in which strange things had happened – the place where he dared not go.

➤ **To create the impression of intelligence** (be careful with this – using long sentences can sometimes make the writer seem **pompous**) – e.g. If, like some people, you find yourself unable to get things right first time, you ought to follow the rules set out by the teacher.

➤ **To build up to a final idea** – e.g. If, instead of spending their money on electrical goods, junk food, new clothes and trips to the cinema, they had saved sensibly with their earnings, they might have had enough money left over to go on holiday.

Write a short, two-word sentence on a large piece of paper, e.g. 'Carl ran'. Underneath it, add one word to make the sentence longer, e.g. 'Carl ran *slowly*'. After that, add two more words to extend the sentence further, e.g. 'Carl ran slowly', *but won*. After that, add three more words to the sentence, and then four – and so on. Keep going until you can add no more words. This can be done individually or in competition with someone.

1. Give an example of a situation where short sentences might be good in descriptive writing.

2. Give an example of where short sentences might be good in informative writing.

3. Give an example of a situation where long sentences might be good in descriptive writing.

4. Give an example of where long sentences might be good in informative writing.

5. Why might a writer have to be careful with using long sentences, according to this module?

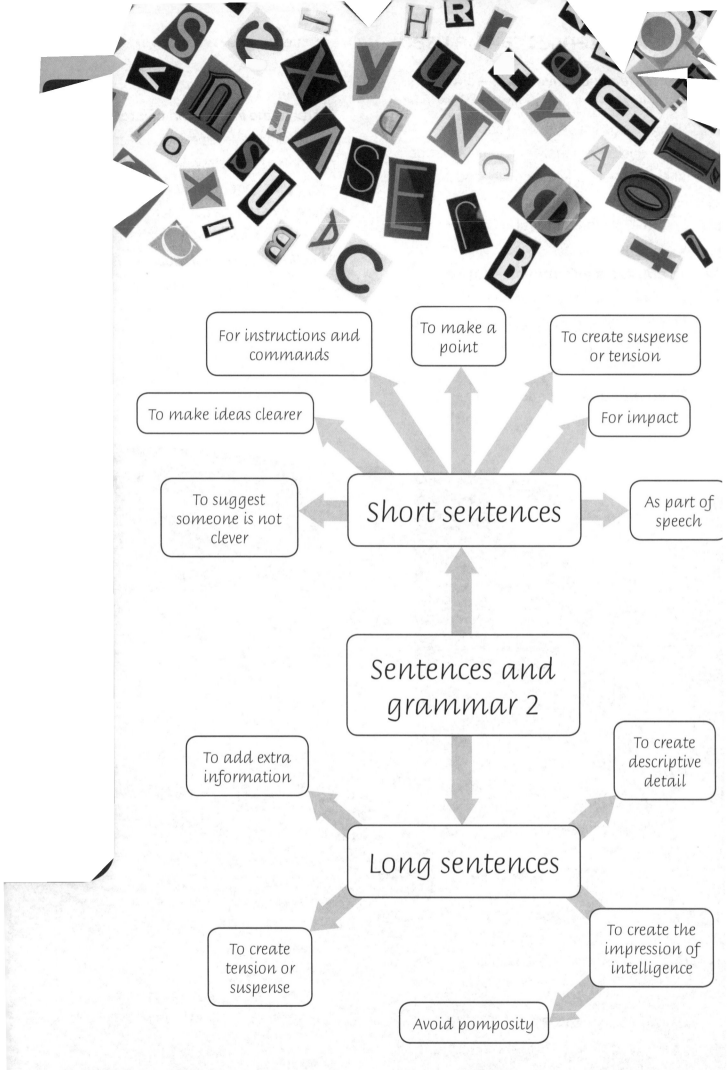

For instructions and commands

To make a point

To create suspense or tension

To make ideas clearer

For impact

To suggest someone is not clever

Short sentences

As part of speech

Sentences and grammar 2

To add extra information

To create descriptive detail

Long sentences

To create tension or suspense

To create the impression of intelligence

Avoid pomposity

Answer the questions below.

1. Write examples of short sentences for the following reasons: (7)

   - To create impact
   - As part of speech
   - To make a point
   - To create suspense or tension
   - To write instructions or give commands
   - To make your ideas clearer
   - To create the impression that someone is not very clever.

2. Write examples of long sentences for the following reasons: (5)

   - To create descriptive detail
   - To add extra information
   - To create tension or suspense
   - To create the impression of intelligence
   - To build up to a final idea.

3. What is the effect or purpose of each example of these short sentences?

   a. Fasten the catch. Turn the key. The lock should now work. (1)

   b. He slipped through. Slowly, he crept in. He held the treasure
   map. This was it! (1)

   c. "Stop! Don't do it! It's dangerous!" (1)

4. What is the effect or purpose of each example of these long sentences?

   a. Before you cook Cajun food, you should get hold of lots of spices
   and also understand that many of the ingredients will be labelled in
   French, as that is the native tongue of many Louisiana citizens. (1)

   b. The dark, gloomy steps led to a vault that smelled of damp and
   decay – the weeds and mould in there had festered and grown
   over the coffins like a creeping fungal infection, throughout many
   sad, dismal and uncelebrated centuries of neglect. (1)

A main difference between written and spoken language is that most written material is intended to be read by someone who is separated from the writer. To communicate successfully, it has to be more carefully crafted than spoken language, because the reader cannot ask the writer for explanations.

Transient ➤
Lasting only for a short time

Features of spoken language

Spoken language is simplified, not so strict about grammar and often brief. It is more sensitive to fashion, social and cultural changes. Some words or expressions are used for a short time but will then disappear or change their meaning. This is even more obvious when it comes to slang, which can change within days or weeks.

➤ *Spoken language is limited by time* – there is only so much you can say in a given time.

➤ *Spoken language is **transient*** – once it is said it is gone (unless it is recorded).

➤ *Spoken language is dynamic* – there are additional features which affect its meaning, such as pace, pitch, intonation, stress, accent, volume, etc.

In spoken language, grammatical errors are often overlooked if the speaker's intentions are understood by the listener.

Features of written language

Written language doesn't change as quickly as spoken language. It is stricter with regards to grammar and **syntax**.

➤ *Written language is limited by space* – there are only so many words you can fit in a given space.

➤ *Written language is permanent* – once written it has to be deliberately erased.

➤ *Written language is static* – there are no additional features such as expression, facial expressions, etc. that might alter its meaning.

In written language, grammatical errors are permanent and less easily forgiven, as the writer, it is assumed, has time to change such errors – if the writer does not correct errors, then the implication can be that they are somehow lazy or lacking in intelligence.

Syntax ➤ Word order

Static ➤ Unmoving, unchanging

Record a short extract – about 30 seconds – from a TV or radio broadcast where someone is holding a conversation. Make a transcript (an exact written copy of what they say) of the speeches. Then re-write it as a) a script, b) a newspaper report. Think about how the same ideas will be worded differently in a written form. What should you take out? What should you put in?

1. What is spoken language not so strict about?
2. How quickly might slang change?
3. Which type of language changes more quickly – written or spoken language?
4. What is written language limited by?
5. Why is written language permanent?

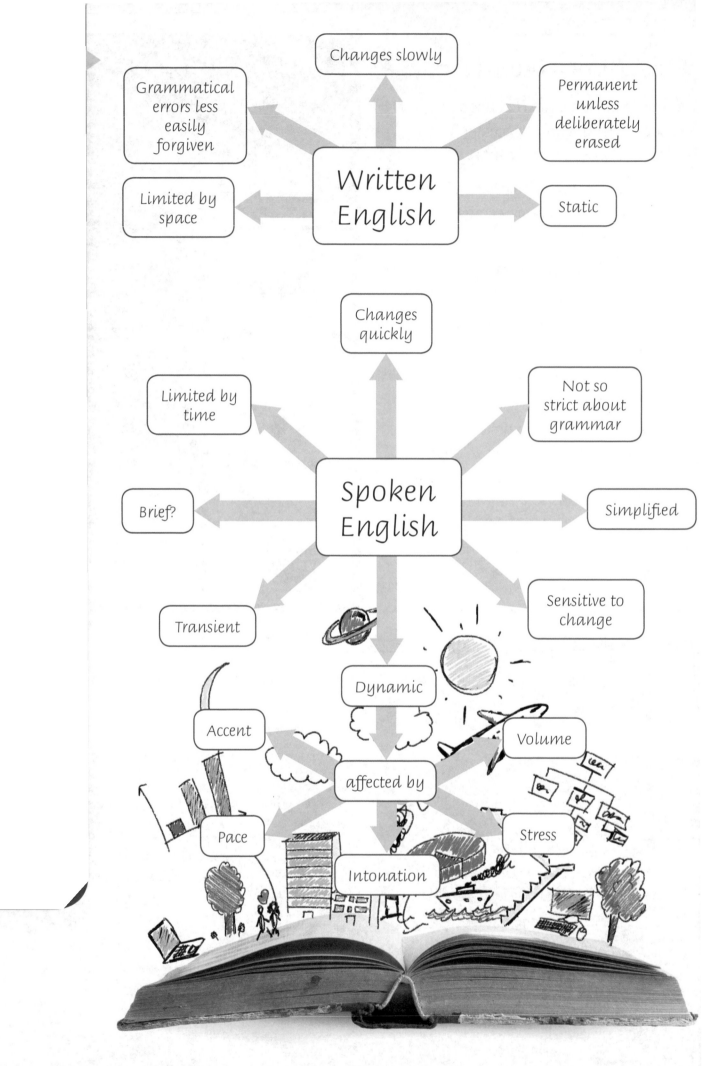

Changes slowly

Grammatical errors less easily forgiven

Permanent unless deliberately erased

Limited by space

Written English

Static

Changes quickly

Limited by time

Not so strict about grammar

Brief?

Spoken English

Simplified

Transient

Sensitive to change

Dynamic

Accent

Volume

affected by

Pace

Stress

Intonation

Below is a glossary of terms used to analyse spoken language. For each one, give an extra example. Use a separate piece of paper to write your answers on. **(16)**

Name of feature	Explanation of feature	First examples
Prosodic features	Elements of spoken language, e.g. sounds	grr
Jargon	Any technical terms belonging to a group (teacher, student, military, job, etc.)	'emotive language' is a technical term – jargon – that teachers use with students, but other people might not understand
Colloquial terms	Close to slang, where people use less formal expressions	'take a hike' (go away)
Formal/informal tone	It can be patronising, friendly, intimate, ironic, over-friendly, formal, distant, etc.	Hello darling, how are you my dearest love?
Back-channelling	This is giving feedback to show that a message/comment has been understood	Yep!
Fillers	Sounds used to fill in gaps in conversation or speech	um, ah, well
Hedge	Where someone softens what they say so as to avoid causing offence or being too direct	I heard that your Aunty had passed away.
Elliptical expression	Missing out words from a sentence – this can also be seen as slang	You done it?
Contractions	Shortened words	'cause (because)
Elision	Blending two words together	howzat? (how's that?)
Subtext	The hidden meaning to a conversation, i.e. the part of the meaning that the speakers don't need to explain	You know what they say about people like that don't you?
Expected greeting	What people usually say when they meet someone	Hi!
Expected sign off	What people usually say when they leave someone	'Bye!
Inclusive language	Words like 'we' or 'us' used to create a group identity or to avoid personal responsibility	We all know what's up, don't we?
Imperative verbs	Command words/instructions – they can be seen as rude or direct	Go!
Subjunctive verbs	Polite forms of making a request (more polite than the imperative)	You might do it?

Standard English

Standard English is the form of the English language that is accepted as the correct form.

It is made up of grammar, vocabulary and spelling, and many believe that it is a close match for written English.

It is also sometimes known as 'The Queen's English' and is associated with the accent called 'Received Pronunciation'.

It is often defined as a version of English that everyone in the country – regardless of their accent or dialect – can understand.

It is virtually impossible to truly define Standard English, as what is standard in one English-speaking country or territory may not match the standard in another country or territory.

Received Pronunciation is regarded by many as a prestigious accent and is associated with success.

Received Pronunciation is a non-regional accent – it can be heard in many parts of many English-speaking areas.

Watch a 30-minute news broadcast. How many accents can you spot in that time?

Accent

Accent is a noticeable way of pronouncing a language, usually associated with, or linked to, a particular country, area or **social class**.

People are often judged and stereotyped, both positively and negatively, based on their accent. For example, in the USA, the British accent is usually regarded as very attractive.

Everyone has an accent of some sort – Received Pronunciation is an accent. There is no such thing as a person who is 'accentless'.

An individual's accent is influenced by: where they grew up ➤ where they travel to ➤ who they grew up with ➤ who they meet ➤ how other people respond to the way they speak.

A person's accent is constantly evolving as they are exposed to new people, attitudes and pronunciations.

United Kingdom

Social class ➤

People who share the same social, economic or educational level or status

Dialect

Dialect is a particular variation of a language which is peculiar to a specific area or group of people, for example, Liverpudlian dialect or Yorkshire dialect or computer workers' dialect.

Dialect is a sub-language of a standard language – for example, Geordie dialect is a sub-language of Standard English. It contains many features of the parent language, but its vocabulary and pronunciation may well be quite different.

Dialect contains its own special words and phrases. These might be used in a specific area, or by a particular group of people. For example, Cockney dialect is spoken by people who were born within earshot of Bow Bells in London.

Accent is a feature of many dialects – for example, Glaswegian dialect is spoken with a strong accent.

Dialect, like accent, is constantly developing as people travel and are exposed to other attitudes and language variations.

As with the issue of accent, many people are judged according to how strong their use of dialect is. This judgement will differ depending on where someone is using the dialect – for example, if they use it away from its natural environment, they may be met with confusion or even hostility, but in its own environment, they will more likely be accepted as 'fitting in'.

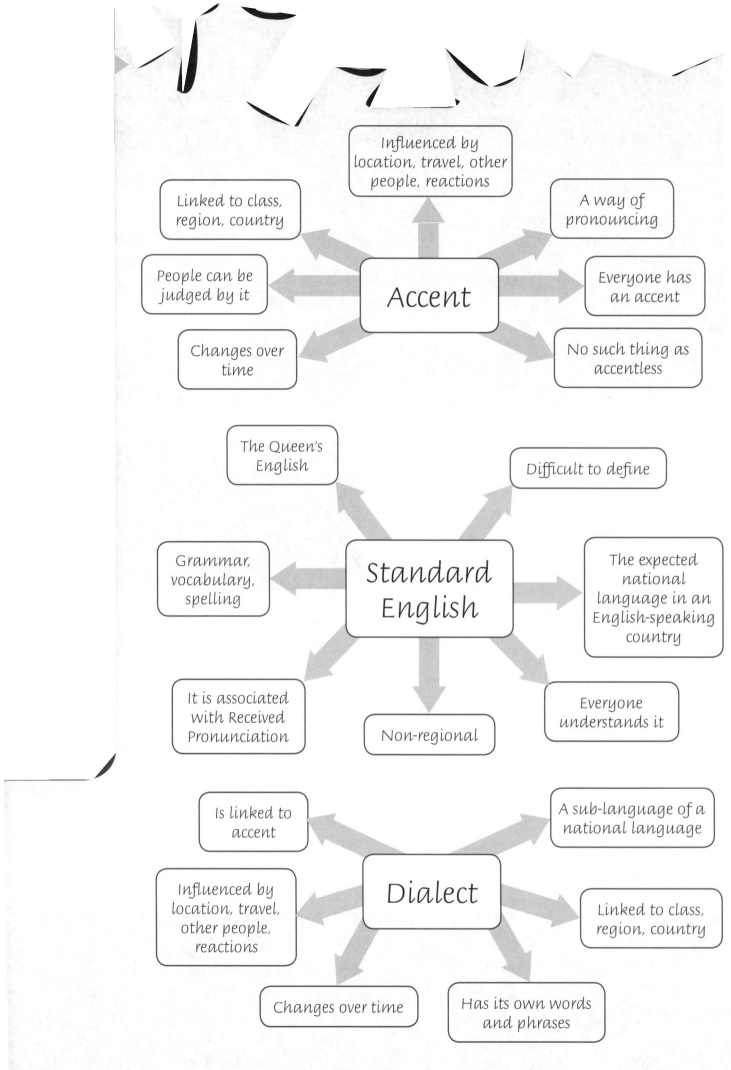

Accent

- Influenced by location, travel, other people, reactions
- Linked to class, region, country
- A way of pronouncing
- People can be judged by it
- Everyone has an accent
- Changes over time
- No such thing as accentless

Standard English

- The Queen's English
- Difficult to define
- Grammar, vocabulary, spelling
- The expected national language in an English-speaking country
- It is associated with Received Pronunciation
- Non-regional
- Everyone understands it

Dialect

- Is linked to accent
- A sub-language of a national language
- Influenced by location, travel, other people, reactions
- Linked to class, region, country
- Changes over time
- Has its own words and phrases

Cockney rhyming slang is a famous dialect. Here are a number of phrases spoken in this dialect. They are not matched up correctly. Match the phrases with their meanings. (24)

Cockney phrase	Standard English meaning
apples and pears	face
baked bean	boots
baker's dozen	dead
Barnet Fair	phone
boat race	kid
bricks and mortar	stink
brown bread	feet
China plate	hair
daisy roots	tea
dog and bone	mate
dustbin lid	mouth
frog and toad	pub
Hampstead Heath	cake
jam jar	cousin
north and south	teeth
pen and ink	wig(s)
plates of meat	wife
Rosie Lee	car
rub-a-dub-dub	road
Sexton Blake	queen
syrup of figs	thief
tea leaf	suit
trouble and strife	stairs
whistle and flute	daughter

Communicating effectively

Ask yourself some questions before you start to plan your speech or presentation.

Who are you going to be talking to?

This will affect your talk in a number of ways.

➤ If you are talking to a group of friends, or people who know you, then this will allow you to be informal.

➤ If you are talking to older people, or in a serious situation, then your speech will have to be more formal – for example, if you are delivering a presentation in Science about how to conduct an experiment.

➤ Also consider how much your audience know about the subject you have to talk about, because that will affect your content.

What are you expected to talk about?

➤ If your audience already know some things about your chosen topic, then don't risk boring them by repeating what they already know.

➤ You will need to research your topic carefully – don't say things that you aren't sure of, because you might get asked questions that you can't answer!

➤ Make some notes that you can refer to later, if you do get asked questions.

Cue cards ➤ Cards that are held during a speech or presentation, to read from, or to give the speaker prompt words about a section of the speech

Pick a hobby or take a random topic chosen by a friend and see if you can talk about it for one minute. Before you start talking, put six words on a cue card, to do with the topic. Try to talk about each of those words for 10 seconds each. If you can, you will end up building up to a minute's speech, quite easily.

22

How long should your talk last?

- You will usually be told this. It is important that you stick to the time you are given. It may be that several other people have to give talks too, or there is only so much time that the talk will fit into.

- In order to make sure you stick to your given time, you will need to practise before.

- Break your talk into sections, and time each section. When you know how long it takes overall, adjust the length of individual sections, rather than try and adjust the whole talk.

What facilities will you have to deliver your talk?

➤ If you are using a slide presentation, don't read off the screen – your audience can hopefully do that without you doing it for them. Instead, talk about the slides you use and add extra information.

➤ Use pictures rather than too much text; pick out details of the images and develop your ideas from these.

➤ If you are not using a slide presentation, then use **cue cards** – but don't read directly off them.

➤ Bring in props and talk about them to support your ideas. This will help to keep the audience's attention.

What is the purpose of your talk?

Are you trying to entertain, inform or perhaps even persuade your audience? This will affect the kinds of things that you say.

➤ If the purpose is to entertain, then your talk might use humour, anecdotes and suitable props.

➤ If the purpose is to inform, then clear structure, appropriate technical vocabulary and sensible organisation will be important.

➤ If the purpose is to persuade, then you might need to use a range of persuasive techniques, such as rhetorical questions, in order to convince the audience that your ideas are correct.

1. Give an example of when you might deliver a more informal speech.

2. Give an example of when you might deliver a more formal speech.

3. What might you use cue cards for?

4. Why should you not read off a screen or whiteboard?

5. How might props help you with your talk?

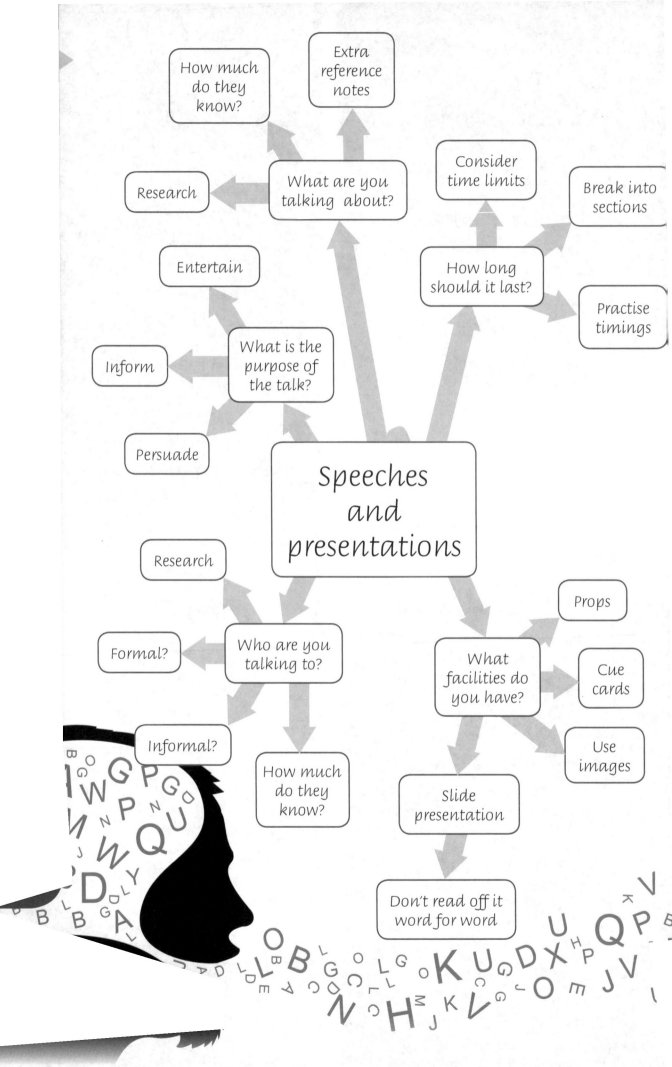

Complete the warm-up exercises.

WARM-UP EXERCISE 1

You are going to see if you can talk for a minute without detailed notes, about your favourite television programme. In order to help you, there are six prompts below. Try to talk for about 10 seconds on each prompt.

1. What it is about.

2. My favourite episode.

3. My favourite character.

4. What I hope will happen in it.

5. What I dislike about it.

6. Why I would recommend it to other people.

Note the time for your first attempt.

Now try it again, but this time, think about how far you got through the prompts and how long you took. If you went over time, reduce how long you spoke on the relevant sections. If you didn't speak for long enough, then try and increase the time on each section.

Note the time for your second attempt.

Keep trying this, until you can speak for as close to one minute as possible.

WARM-UP EXERCISE 2

Choose a topic of your own choice. Write six, one-word prompts and then repeat the exercise above, to see if you can plan a talk and not rely on detailed notes.

WARM-UP EXERCISE 3

Choose a picture with no text on it. Label six things in the photograph. Try to talk for one minute about the photograph, without repeating yourself, using only the labels that you have put on it. This will help you to talk without reading off a script.

Module 1

Quick questions

1. Stories were only just being written down for the first time.
2. They used alliteration and rhymes.
3. Chaucer, Malory.
4. 16th and 17th centuries.
5. Wrote in a wide variety of styles. Huge impact on the English language. Wrote about all classes of people.

Practice questions

1. Farming, making gloves, dealing in wool, local officer.
2. Of good reputation.
3. An important local job, possibly a councillor or similar.
4. 'Some historians have suggested that he went away to London because he did not get on with his wife.'
5. 3, 1, 4, 2   (4; 1 mark for each paragraph)

Module 2

Quick questions

1. You will see more new words and learn more about them.
2. A group of letters added to the start of a word to modify its meaning.
3. The base word, after all extra parts have been removed.
4. To learn new vocabulary and concepts.
5. It will confirm any ideas you have about the meanings of new words.

Practice questions

1. A   6. A
2. B   7. B
3. B   8. B
4. A   9. C
5. C   10. B

Module 3

Quick questions

1. Your reading goes beyond straightforward understanding.
2. Question the texts in front of you.
3. They might tell you something about the mood or attitude of the characters.
4. They will also help you to work out the mood or attitude of the characters.
5. Questions will lead to understanding and then lead to more questions and deeper understanding.

Practice questions

There are various answers to this exercise. Here are some suggestions.

1. Facts alone are wanted in life	Why does the speaker say this? Why sort of character does this suggest he has?	It suggests that he's very opinionated and a bit dull.
2. The scene was a plain, bare, monotonous vault of a schoolroom	What does this suggest about the children's environment and education?	Both were dull and boring and unwelcoming.
3. the speaker's square wall of a forehead	Why is the speaker's head so unnatural?	The speaker is obstinate and unwelcoming.
4. the speaker's voice, which was inflexible, dry, and dictatorial	Why does he speak in this way?	He is fixed in his ways and does not want to change his mind. He is narrow-minded.

5. like the crust of a plum pie	What picture does this simile create?	It makes the man's head seem rather ridiculous and so it makes the man seem ridiculous.

Module 4

Quick questions

1. Stories might be written for newspapers in instalments, so the author might use cliffhangers, like Dickens.
2. Yes. A person might be writing for their own entertainment.
3. Entertain, shock, make people laugh, make money, work out their own thoughts and feelings.
4. It might affect their opinions or point of view.
5. Writers might fit in with fashions or rebel against them.

Practice questions

1. She had romance in her life.
2. She wrote about what she knew.
3. She maybe wrote to express her feelings.

Module 5

Quick questions

1. Situation, who speaks, context, how the words are spoken.
2. Similes, metaphors, personification, pathetic fallacy.
3. Onomatopoeia, alliteration, sibilance, fricatives, assonance.
4. How characters are written and presented to portray certain ideas.
5. Biography, diary, letter, romance, science fiction are named in the passage. Other acceptable answers possible.

Practice questions

1. First person.
2. "sheer scale of the skyscrapers" – creates a soaring feeling to suggest height. "angry, aggravated and anxious" – suggests moodiness. "as I wandered around, almost anonymously" – suggests the writer is hidden.
3. Opinions, descriptive techniques, emotions, a range of senses.
4. Various answers possible – any two parts of the first paragraph could be quoted to suggest that the writer feels overcome.
   Most of the second paragraph could be quoted and comments made on the contrasts in the city.
   The third paragraph could be used to make comments about the city as a drama.   (2; 1 mark for each phrase)
5. Past tense.
6. Conversational, informal, chatty style. It makes the reader feel as though they are close to the writer and privy to his thoughts and feelings. Various quotations could be used to support this idea. One example would be from the first sentence: "I'd seen nothing quite like this city, even though I'd read about it and seen it on so many films."   (3; 1 mark for naming style, 1 mark for explaining the effect and 1 mark for a valid quotation)

Module 6

Quick questions

1. Iambic, trochaic, spondaic, anapestic, dactylic.
2. Iambic, trochaic, spondaic.
3. Anapestic, dactylic.
4. A rhyme in which the stress is on the final syllable of the words.

5. A rhyme in which the stress is on the second from last syllable of the words.

Practice questions

1. a. Ten. **b.** Eight. **c.** It means rhythm. **d.** Two syllables, with only the first stressed. **e.** Three syllables, with only the third stressed. **f.** One stressed syllable followed by two unstressed. **g.** Two consecutive syllables that are both stressed. **h.** Spondee. **i.** Iambic pentameter. **j.** Trochaic. **k.** Spondaic. **l.** Dactylic.

2. a. AABBA **b.** ABCB

Module 7

Quick questions

1. Short stories, factual prose, letters, novels, diaries, testimony, journals, personal essays. (All could have some degree of imagination, including the factual ones.)
2. Scripts, comedy, tragedy, one-act plays, pantomimes are mentioned in the module.
3. Acrostic, ballad, blank verse, epic poems, epigrams, free verse, haiku, kennings, limericks, lyrics, odes, shape poems, sonnets.
4. Active.
5. Passive.

Practice questions

1. Limerick – Short, five-line AABBA humorous poem; Horror novel – Dark settings, references to evil and the supernatural; Love sonnet – 14-line poem usually written by an admirer; Melodramatic play – A play with extravagant action and emotion; Science fiction novel – A novel that may involve futuristic ideas; Pantomime – A humorous play traditionally involving audience participation; Tragic play – A play that has a very sad ending; Fictional biography – A novel that tells the life story of an imaginary person or character; Ballad – A story-poem, usually of some length; Romance novel – A novel that may involve emotions of attraction.
2. Most likely answers: **a.** The carrots were eaten by the boy. **b.** The homework was done by the girl. **c.** The song was sung by the singer. **d.** The mistakes were crossed out by the writer. **e.** The ball was kicked by the footballer.
3. Most likely answers: **a.** The manager accepted the result. **b.** The bad weather closed the school. **c.** The gardener chopped the tree down. **d.** The celebrity chef cooked the meal. **e.** The engineer switched off the television.
4. **a.** Prose. **b.** Poetry. **c.** Prose. **d.** Prose. **e.** Prose.

Module 8

Quick questions

1. Business letters, job applications, letters of complaint, instructions, educational or reference books, information texts, academic essays, reports.
2. Clear writing, literal, well-structured and organised, suitable vocabulary for audience, likely to be in the passive voice.
3. Different institutions have different house styles for letters. Letter writing conventions have changed over time and are still changing.
4. An introduction which addresses the issue to be discussed.
5. A series of points developing a line of argument.

Practice questions

1. G – The postal code is missing.
2. E – The date is missing.
3. A – Shortened version of the recipient's address is missing. (Dependent on house style, Answers 2 and 3 could be swapped and be correct.)
4. H – The salutation is too informal.
5. K – The style of the body text is too informal.
6. D – The closing is too informal.
7. J – The signature is missing.

Module 9

Quick questions

Answers given in the module. Other answers may be valid.

1. Quick and easy, good for short responses, OK for tasks that require straightforward, simple responses.
2. Straightforward, logical order, easily numbered, good for sequencing ideas.
3. Good for generating ideas/working at speed.
4. Good for sequence and development of ideas.
5. Can be moved around and re-ordered.

Practice questions

A variety of answers are possible here. Answers below are likely suggestions.

1. Each point should correspond to a paragraph in the essay.
2. Lists lend themselves to sequencing more easily, whereas mind-maps scatter ideas and would have to be numbered.
3. A mind-map would allow for greater development and expansion of ideas and show a train of thought.
4. Sticky notes could be easily re-sequenced when putting ideas into chronological order.
5. There is too much detailed information to safely commit to memory.

Module 10

Quick questions

1. A primary audience can be more easily controlled and influenced than an unknown secondary audience.
2. Secondary audiences could be anybody, so their responses are difficult to predict.
3. Register is the degree or level of formality in a written text. It is important because, if it is not pitched correctly, the reader could take offence.
4. To entertain, describe, explain, analyse, comment, review, advise, inform, persuade, argue, instruct.
5. Language, viewpoint, register, tone, vocabulary, sentence types.

Practice questions

1. **a.** Action-adventure. **b.** Romance. **c.** Fantasy. Primary purpose is to entertain. (3; 1 mark for each extract)
2. **a.** Students – possibly teachers. **b.** Tourists. **c.** Someone whose washing machine has broken and who wishes to fix it.
3. Exaggerated, simple vocabulary – Child's comic book; Short, step-by-step sentences – A quick guide to setting up a TV; Complex, descriptive sentences – Adult novel; A second-person persuasive style – An advert; Lots of obscure specialist technical vocabulary – An instruction manual for complex machinery.

Module 11

Quick questions

1. Tell some sort of story.
2. Deal with cause and effect/have a main idea and supporting details/alphabetical order/usually non-fiction, but don't have to be.
3. A parody of a fictional non-fiction text, or a humorous dictionary are mentioned in the module. Other answers may be possible and valid.
4. Argumentative essay/school textbook are mentioned in the module – other answers may be possible and valid.
5. Purpose? Will it be re-read and used as reference? Is it developing an argument/discussing a range of ideas? Does it belong to a particular genre?

Practice questions

1. The first reason why I love folk music is…
2. The next reason why I like folk music is…
3. Thirdly, the stories that are told in folk music are fascinating…
4. A different reason why I like folk music is that it is unfashionable at this moment in time…
5. In contrast to this, I feel that folk music offers tremendous opportunities to find out about our past…
6. A further reason why I like folk music is that it can be enjoyed anywhere…
7. My seventh reason is a personal one – there are many performers and singers whose voices and choice of songs really appeal to me…

8. Eighth on my list of reasons is the fact that attending folk music concerts is really cheap…
9. This leads on to my ninth and penultimate point, the fact that when you are at a folk music concert, you will be close to the people making the music…
10. Finally, I realise that folk music is not for everyone…

Module 12
Quick questions
1. If you are working in a group or as part of a team, someone else in the group or team. Other answers possible not listed in the module.
2. Put title and date/don't limit length of notes/leave spaces/use one colour pen when listening to save time/colour-code when reading/spider diagrams and mind-maps are good to do when reading/don't write sentences in full/make sure you will understand them later/record a speaker, with permission.
3. Coloured paper/file dividers/label and number sheets/make an index.
4. Use smartphone apps/have a folder system on a computer/back up files.
5. If you don't back up files, you could lose them all.

Practice questions
1. Various answers possible.
   Key dates: 1979 (birth); 1997 (left school); 2004 (began music career); 2008 (won a competition)   (4; 1 mark for each date)
   Key skills: Music photography; compositional skills; awareness of colour; kinaesthetic skills; ability to play a musical instrument/use a camera; modelling ability;   (6; 1 mark for each key skill)
   Most famous events: Gained national exposure in 'Photography International'; Won a National Youth Music competition; Chosen by 'Pongofoot Trainer Insoles' to be a model   (3; 1 mark for each famous event)
2. Many different responses possible. No set answer. Answers should be around 118 words and include a range of key facts.   (200-236 words = 1 mark; 175-199 words = 2 marks; 160-174 words = 3 marks; 145-159 words = 4 marks; 118-144 words = 5 marks)

Module 13
Quick questions
1. To intrigue and create interest.
2. Adjectives – soft, wavy, coastal. Adverbs – longingly, gently (x2), thoughtfully, completely.
3. Find/ensure/insert.
4. 'There was only one thing to do and that was to go back again to the dark, sad house…'
5. Do I want to reveal everything? Do I want to leave some things to the imagination of the reader? Will there be a sequel? Do I want to shock, surprise or cause other feelings?

Practice questions
1. Various responses possible. Good answers will include all the features in the prompts. (19; 1 mark for each correct answer)
2. Buried/experts/hoard/quoted/ancient. (5; 1 mark for each correct answer)
3. Various responses possible. Good answers will include all the features in the prompts. (10; 1 mark for each correct answer)

Module 14
Quick questions
1. Write all your ideas out in one go and then change them afterwards. Write your ideas out and change them as you go along.

2. Is the text of a consistent standard? Is the whole piece balanced?
3. Make sure that a dictionary has been used alongside the spellcheck to ensure that the correct words have been chosen, especially with homophones.
4. its/it's.
5. Computer software programs tend not to notice whether homophones have been used correctly or not – they detect spellings, not meanings.

Practice questions
1. Corrections are highlighted.
   Since visiting Haworth in West Yorkshire, I have been intrigued by the Brontë Sisters, which has further led to a passion for English Literature in general. Experiencing the inspirational scenery for the various novels has caused me to revel in finding links between writers and their texts, as well as finding a personal connection with a novel and the writer. I find *Wuthering Heights* in particular a captivating novel, which I have enthusiastically studied at A-level. However, my favourite novel would have to be To Kill a Mockingbird, by Harper Lee, which I found to be sensationally thought-provoking. For me, what makes English Literature such an inspiring and appealing subject to study is not just the impact that books leave on a person, but the varying opinions and alternative interpretations that spring from reading them. I have a desire to develop and expand my knowledge of literary genres, key literary movements and the techniques used by writers to communicate a message or meaning. In class, I actively contribute to discussions and debates, as well as having a fascination with the purposes and personal aims of writers. Being on the college Student Council has further improved my confidence when talking to unfamiliar people and I have been able to voice my opinion, without causing conflict.   (14)
   a. This would create a bad impression/suggest that the student was careless/lacking in quality.
   b. The application would more than likely be unsuccessful, as the mistakes relate to English skills and this is an English course that is being applied for.
2. Corrections are highlighted.
   While I was living in Stoke-on-Trent, there were many things that I liked. One thing that I liked was the food. Oatcakes are a speciality of the area and lots of people eat them every day. You can buy them from oatcake shops which you don't get anywhere else in the country. It's a shame that they are not available anywhere else in Britain, as I am sure that many people would like them. (10)

Module 15
Quick questions
1. Spell-speak/words within words/count syllables/mnemonics/learn root words/learn spelling rules.
2. If a word ends in a consonant plus 'y', change the 'y' to 'i', before adding any ending, e.g. country – countries.
3. When 'c' is followed by 'e', 'i' or 'y', it sounds like 's'.
4. 'ti', 'ci', 'si', are three pairs of letters used to say 'sh'.
5. Most words that end in the letter 'f' become plural by adding the suffix 'ves'.

Practice questions
1. a. Rasspberry / Raspberry / Razberry
   b. Februay / Februery / February
   c. Necessity / Neccessity / Neccessaty
   d. Libary / Librery / Library
   e. Naybor / Neighbour / Nieghbour
   f. Rumour / Rumer / Roomor

g. ~~Adress~~ / Address / ~~Adress~~

h. ~~Dissappoint~~ / Disappoint / ~~Disapoint~~

i. ~~Greatful~~ / ~~Greitful~~ / Grateful

j. ~~Hypocrissy~~ / Hypocrisy / ~~Hypocrassy~~

2. a. The food was <u>appalling</u>.

b. I am going <u>travelling</u> before I go to university.

c. Michelle decided to dress <u>formally</u> for the ball.

d. I <u>usually</u> shop here.

e. "Do you live <u>locally</u>?"

3. a. I <u>admitted</u> my guilt to the court yesterday.

b. Sheila <u>regretted</u> her actions.

c. I <u>benefited</u> from last week's exercise.

d. I <u>visited</u> my relations last month.

e. I have <u>committed</u> no crime.

4. a. The man was waiting at the <u>station</u>.

b. Everyone sang the <u>national</u> anthem.

c. "Don't waste my <u>precious</u> time!"

d. <u>Possession</u> is nine-tenths of the law.

e. The class didn't understand <u>fractions</u> in their Maths lesson.

Module 16
Quick questions
1. Yes.
2. Yes.
3. Complex lists.
4. Quotations and speeches.
5. No.

Practice questions
1. a. I am going home; I will set out from there.

b. It rained heavily; we still went for our walk.

c. It was too dark; we couldn't finish the trip.

d. I am going home; moreover, I will set out from there.

e. It rained heavily; however, we still went for our walk.

f. It was too rich; we couldn't eat it.

g. We finished the exercise; the test was over.

h. There were many different people: the enthusiastic youngsters; the veteran performers; the weekend amateurs; all were taking part.

2. Various answers possible. Check against the criteria given in the module. (10; 1 mark for each correctly punctuated sentence)

3. a. There were only two things that Fred worried about: where the colon went and why it was used.

b. He only needed one thing to get through the week: money.

c. Rule number one: the teacher is always right.

d. Everything went right on that day: they won the lottery; the electricity came back on; Jane got a new job and their pet dog was found.

e. The teacher spoke: "Pens down and pay attention to what I am going to say."

f. I enjoy reading: novels by Jane Austen are among my favourites.

g. There is only one thing left to do now: confess while you still have time.

h. You are left with only one option: keep going until you have got it right.

4. Various answers possible. Check against the criteria given in the module. (10; 1 mark for each correctly punctuated sentence)

Module 17
Quick questions
1. Omission – leaving something out.
2. Possession – belonging.
3. Can't – cannot. It stands for the missing 'n' and 'o'.
4. One.
5. Several.

Practice questions
1. a. Saffron couldn't believe that she had got the question wrong.

b. Dean hadn't done his homework.

c. Kayleigh shouldn't have eaten all the cakes.

d. "I've got it!" shouted Ryan.

e. "Where's the exit?" asked Abigail.

f. Kim didn't understand what she had been asked to do.

g. "I could've done that!" remarked Mr Rachid.

h. Joe should've been smarter when he went for his interview.

i. "Where'd Jake go?" asked Jack.

j. "Lucy won't do the reading," explained Miss Sowter.

2. Various answers possible. Check against the rules given in the module. (10; 1 mark for each correctly punctuated sentence)

3. a. Joe's Pub is in New York.

b. Nobody understood why Oliver's answer was wrong.

c. Luke's bag had broken.

d. Matthew was distracted by Laura's chatter.

e. Poppy's pen had been taken by Sadie.

f. Syed and Charlie's work was better than expected.

g. James' excuse for not doing his homework wasn't accepted by the teacher.

h. Lots of girls' teams took part in the tournament.

i. The girl's bag was returned to her.

j. Frances' grade was the best in the class.

4. Various answers possible. Check against the rules given in the module. (10; 1 mark for each correctly punctuated sentence)

Module 18
Quick questions
1. The main part of a sentence.
2. A part of a sentence that doesn't make sense on its own – it depends on the main clause for its meaning.
3. It changes.
4. Three in this module – although there could be more.
5. When you write, consider which part of the sentence you want to emphasise, or whether you want to build up tension, or create surprise.

Practice questions
1. Main clause is highlighted. (2; 1 mark for main clause, 1 mark for subordinate clause)

a. Becky didn't do her homework, because she had lost her book. (2)

b. Sadie said that she understood the work, which was unusual for her. (2)

c. Jake put his head on the desk, because he was tired. (2)

d. Despite being a well-behaved boy, Alex was moved by the teacher. (2)

e. Although she had been away, Laura got top marks in the exam. (2)

f. Sara laughed, because Sophie dropped her sweets. (2)

g. Emily's work was good, despite her being untidy. (2)

h. Although he was Head boy, Jack was a disruptive influence. (2)

i. Tyler revised thoroughly, because he wanted to succeed. (2)

j. Because she had a cold, Courtney was absent. (2)

2. a. Because she had lost her book, Becky didn't do her homework.

b. It was unusual for Sadie, but she said she understood the work.

c. Because he was tired, Jake put his head on the desk.

d. Alex was moved by the teacher, even though he was a well-behaved boy.

e. Laura got top marks in the exam, even though she had been away.

f. Because Sophie dropped her sweets, Sara laughed.

g. Despite her being untidy, Emily's work was good.

h. Jack was a disruptive influence, even though he was Head boy.

i. Because he wanted to succeed, Tyler revised thoroughly.

j. Courtney was absent, because she had a cold.

3. The main clause is in yellow and the other subordinate clauses are in green and blue. (2; 1 mark for main clause, 1 mark for subordinate clause)

a. Although he was very young, Grant was a great musician, who many people admired. (2)

b. Mike loved painting, because it gave him an extra income, despite his teaching job. (2)

c. Although his children didn't like it, Gerald's beard grew, because he didn't shave it. (2)

d. Robbie wrote down all his ideas, although they were only rough, because he liked to draft his work. (2)

e. Donna, although she was a married woman, worked away from her family. (2)

f. Preston, despite being the name of a place, was also a boy's name. (2)

g. Chicago, one of the largest cities in America, was home to the Fulks family. (2)

h. Tara and Rob, parents of Clayton, managed to pay for his (Clayton's) education. (2)

i. Despite the cold weather, Ed went to work, but got stuck on the way there. (2)

j. Whenever they sang together, despite not liking each other, the couple had success. (2)

4. There are several possible answers for this section. One possible example is given for each, but there are more.

a. Grant was a great musician, who many people admired, even though he was very young.

b. Mike, despite his teaching job, loved painting, because it gave him extra income.

c. Gerald's beard grew, even though his children didn't like it, because he didn't shave it.

d. Because he liked to draft his work, Robbie wrote down all his ideas, even though they were only rough.

e. Donna worked away from her family, even though she was a married woman.

f. Preston was a boy's name, despite being the name of a place.

g. Chicago, home to the Fulks family, was one of the largest cities in America.

h. The parents of Clayton, Tara and Rob, managed to pay for his education.

i. Ed went to work, despite the cold weather, but got stuck on the way there.

j. Despite not liking each other, the couple had success whenever they sang together.

Module 19

Quick questions

1. Create impact/as part of speech/to create suspense or tension/to create an impression of someone not being clever.

2. To make a point/to write instructions or give commands/to make ideas clearer.

3. To create descriptive detail/to create tension or suspense.

4. To add extra information/to create the impression of intelligence.

5. To avoid seeming pompous.

Practice questions

1. Many variations possible – check them against the criteria given in the module. (7; 1 mark for each correctly written sentence)

2. Many variations possible – check them against the criteria given in the module. (7; 1 mark for each correctly written sentence)

3. a. To give information clearly.
   b. To create suspense/tension.
   c. To create shock in a speech and a sense of danger.

4. a. To add informative detail.
   b. To build up tension and suspense.

Module 20

Quick questions

1. Grammar.

2. Weekly or even daily.

3. Spoken.

4. Space.

5. Written language is permanent – once written it has to be deliberately erased.

Practice questions

Many different answers are possible. These are suggestions.

Name of feature	Further example
Prosodic features	hmmm
Jargon	All singing from the same hymn sheet
Colloquial terms	Get lost!
Formal/informal tone	Greetings, oh most honourable master.
Back-channelling	OK
Fillers	Erm… well…
Hedge	I'm going to the ladies' room to powder my nose.
Elliptical expression	What happen?
Contractions	Who's there?
Elision	Who's – who is
Subtext	That's it then?
Expected greeting	Hello!
Expected sign off	't'ra
Inclusive language	It's not our fault is it?
Imperative verbs	Begone!
Subjunctive verbs	You could consider it.

Module 21

Quick questions

1. Grammar, vocabulary and spelling.

2. Yes.

3. Accent is usually associated with, or linked to, a particular country, area or social class.

4. An individual's accent is influenced by where they grew up, where they travel to, who they grew up with, who they meet and how other people respond to the way they speak. A person's accent is constantly evolving as they are exposed to new people, attitudes and pronunciations.

5. Dialect, like accent, is constantly developing as people travel and are exposed to other attitudes and language variations.

Practice questions

apples and pears – stairs; baked bean – queen; baker's dozen – cousin; Barnet Fair – hair; boat race – face; bricks and mortar – daughter; brown bread – dead; China plate – mate; daisy roots – boots; dog and bone – phone; dustbin lid – kid; frog and toad – road; Hampstead Heath – teeth; jam jar – car; north and south – mouth; pen and ink – stink; plates of meat – feet; Rosie Lee – tea; rub-a-dub-dub – pub; Sexton Blake – cake; syrup of figs – wig(s); tea leaf – thief; trouble and strife – wife; whistle and flute – suit.

Module 22

Quick questions

1. If you are talking to a group of friends, or people who know you.

2. If you are talking to older people, or in a serious situation.

3. To read from, or to give a speaker prompt words about a section of a speech.

4. It bores the audience, because they can read it for themselves.

5. They will support your ideas. This will help to keep the audience's attention.

Practice questions

All tasks are for practice only.